# TRANS AND DISABLED

*of related interest*

**Non-Binary Lives**
**An Anthology of Intersecting Identities**
*Edited by Jos Twist, Ben Vincent, Meg-John Barker and Kat Gupta*
ISBN 978 1 78775 339 6
eISBN 978 1 78775 340 2

**Surviving Transphobia**
*Edited by Laura A. Jacobs, LCSW-R*
ISBN 978 1 78775 965 7
eISBN 978 1 78775 966 4

**Spectrums**
**Autistic Transgender People in Their Own Words**
*Edited by Maxfield Sparrow*
ISBN 978 1 78775 014 2
eISBN 978 1 78775 015 9

# Trans and Disabled

## An Anthology of Identities and Experiences

EDITED BY

## Alex Iantaffi

**Jessica Kingsley Publishers**
London and Philadelphia

First published in Great Britain in 2025 by Jessica Kingsley Publishers
An imprint of John Murray Press

1

This book is dedicated to Nila Gupta with love & gratitude.

Wishing you were still here to share your
brilliant creativity with the world,

to laugh & cry late into the night & to have the
hard conversations with all those you love(d).

# Contents

## Part 3: Loving Ourselves and Each Other

# Acknowledgements

First of all, I want to thank each contributor for their vulnerability, brilliance and existence. Thank you for your creativity, your willingness to share it with the world and for contributing to this anthology. This book would literally not exist without you.

I would like to thank my beloved writing partner, Meg-John Barker, for encouraging me to put my work out into the world even (especially) when I feel wobbly. As always, none of my work would be possible without my wonderful nesting partners, Michael Wright and Root Holden, who take on much of the labor of cleaning, cooking, parenting and caring for our animal companions so that I can work, create and write. Thank you for all you do! I couldn't do a third of what I do without you! And thank you to my best friend, Dr. Daz Saunders, for nearly three decades of deep friendship, a history of shared rituals and travels, and love and care across time and space. I feel very blessed to have all of you amazing people believing in me! Thank you.

I am also honored to have two amazing children who keep teaching me to dismantle ableism within myself, each and every day. Thank you for being the wonderful beings that you are. I love you so much.

Finally, I want to express immense gratitude to my editor, Alex DiFrancesco. This was the first time I worked with Alex, and they were incredibly patient and supportive of the numerous times I had to push our deadlines out, due to moving deeply in and through crip time nowadays. Thank you so much, Alex. Your understanding and kindness helped me move through the shame, the internalized ableism and the unrelenting imposter's syndrome that plague my days as I manage decreasing mobility and capacity. Thank you.

# Introduction

When Covid-19 started, one of the many challenging things I faced was explaining to (cisgender and/or abled) people why I was scared to end up in a hospital as a trans and disabled person with a non-English accent who was, to add the cherry on top, not yet a citizen in the country where I lived. This was before tests and vaccines. When we were being told loudly that "we" had nothing to worry about because only "the disabled and the elderly" risked dying. Those of us who were both disabled and trans didn't need to explain this to one another. We knew that if it came to not enough respirators, our lives might be viewed as (more) disposable. We knew that when the media said "we," we were not included. Many Indigenous, Black, Brown and Asian folks knew this too, of course, whether they were trans and/or disabled themselves or not, because they too are usually not part of the "we" that the media refers to when talking about the "general population."

The "general population," against whom psychological and medical tests are far too often normed, for whom curricula are developed in education and who tend to be overly represented in media, are generally white, cisgender, often heterosexual, monogamous, on the wealthier side and most certainly not disabled. Covid-19 didn't create these disparities: it just highlighted with the boldest marker possible who was considered worthy of living under capitalism and colonialism and who wasn't. Those of us who are trans and disabled already knew we weren't being counted in the "worthy" column, although some of us who benefited from white privilege might have still been hiding behind that illusion.

To be trans and disabled is to have experienced being questioned about our status. It means having questioned ourselves whether we are "enough" of one or the other or both identities. To be trans and disabled means to have experienced harassment, discrimination, loneliness, often poverty, and to have struggled with feeling worthy of love, from anyone, including ourselves. It means to have our trans status questioned because of our disabilities and to have our disabilities "blamed" on our trans status. To be trans and disabled sometimes means experiencing ableism within our trans communities and transphobia within our disabled communities. We know how lonely it can feel to briefly glimpse into belonging only to have that ripped from us by a casually hurtful phrase or glance. To be trans and disabled means to love our fellow trans and disabled people harder than we could ever love ourselves.

All this and more is in this anthology. In these pages, you will find vulnerable stories, poems, drawings and personal essays exploring what it means to be us, to make sense of ourselves, our intersections of identities and experiences, of how we are treated, of how quickly everything can change and how much love we are capable of, sometimes even for ourselves. I cried as I read each piece submitted with trust and care by my fellow trans and disabled authors. I cried not because I felt sorry for us but because I am in awe of our words, our stories, our pain, our love and our undeniable beauty. My heart wrapped around each word, each story, some more resonant than others, of course, some almost alien, yet all connected by threads of community and care.

I offer this labyrinth of experiences to you readers, and I hope that you too find, at each turn, a moment to pause and appreciate each one. I have organized this anthology in three parts: who we are; being (treated) different; loving ourselves and each other. These parts are not distinct and separate. Each bleeds and weaves with the others because to be trans and disabled is about identity, but it's also about change, about the ways we are treated as different and struggle to see ourselves as worthy because of it sometimes, and, above all, it's about how we survive (if we're lucky) just long enough to offer one another love and community.

If you're reading this as a cisgender person and/or an abled person, please do not look for inspiration here or for our courage and resilience; this is not what our lives are for, and neither are these pages. I hope, however, that you can find expansion within your mind and heart through these pages. If you're reading this as a trans and disabled person, I hope you find pieces of you in these pages, no matter how small, and if you feel lonely or isolated, maybe these pages might help you feel a little less so. In the end, I wanted this book to exist because many of us are both trans and disabled due to the overlap of systems of oppression, among other things, and too many of us are gone before we can even share our stories. This anthology is not enough. There are still so many more experiences not encompassed within these pages. So many more stories, poems, drawings and plays. I hope you seek them out. And, to my fellow trans and disabled people, I hope we keep finding each other, and loving each other, and being a harbor for one another. To those of you who are already ancestors, I give my eternal gratitude. I am and we are because you were. Thank you.

# PART 1

# WHO WE ARE

# Plural, trans and disabled

(TEAM) MEG-JOHN BARKER

Alex suggested that we might like to write something about plurality for this collection, given that we are a plural system and we're also both trans and disabled. Our plan in this piece is to explore the links between plurality and disability, and between plurality and trans, before ending with some thoughts towards a trans-affirmative, disability justice-inspired framework for plurality.

As well as speaking from a position of *being* plural, we take a plural *perspective* here. In addition to sharing our own lived experience of plurality as it relates to disability and trans, we try to hold space open as far as possible to encompass *all* experiences and understandings of plurality, disability and trans. Let's start with plurality.

## Plurality

For us, plurality means that we experience ourselves—vividly—as five selves within the same selves-system (which is often called Meg-John Barker). The five of us overlap in some ways, but are also quite different from each other—for example, in how we speak and move our bodies, in what we enjoy doing, in the memories and feelings we hold, and in our strengths and limitations. We're all aware of each other now and have loving relationships. However, it took a lifetime of 50 years to get to this point of being fully aware of our plurality, and an intense period of work over the last five years before all of us felt completely welcome here. For more on our specific experience and understanding of plurality, check out the zines referenced at the end of this piece.

Our overall definition of plurality would be that it encompasses *any* experience of being composed of more than one self, soul, part or whatever other word people want to use for it. We'll stick with "selves" here for consistency, but please do feel free to transpose another word if it works better for you. Experiences of plurality may be anywhere on a spectrum from a vague—somewhat metaphorical—sense of inner multiplicity to having several vividly distinct selves. There may be any number of selves, up to infinity. These may be relatively stable or they may change a lot, with selves emerging or merging over time. The person, or system, may or may not *identify* as plural to themselves and/or the world. The selves may or may not have awareness of each other.

We draw on many different plural literatures and related communities in our understandings of plurality. We find something of value in all of them, while we're not always aligned with them in every single way. It's very important to us to hold open the plurality of possible understandings, experiences and expressions of plurality, and to challenge any attempt to suggest that one understanding, experience or expression is more valid than another. If no part gets left behind (Fisher, 2019), then neither does any experience of plurality.

Now let's apply a plural perspective to the ways in which

plurality relates to disability and trans issues. In both these sections, we'll talk about our personal experience and attempt to include other experiences which overlap with, and differ from, our own. Some might experience their plurality as a disability and/or as related to being trans; some may not. So this can differ *between* people or at different points in the same person's life. It may depend on what each of these words means to them, which relates to what they mean in their wider communities and culture/s, all of which may also change over time. Different selves *within* a system may also have different experiences, or opinions, on this.

We find it helpful, where possible, to hold all these perspectives together, however paradoxical or contradictory they may seem. Rather than the oppositional questions of whether or not plurality is a form of disability, or whether or not plurality is a form of trans (or vice versa), it can be more useful to ask what opens up when we consider plurality as a form of disability or trans, and also what closes down (Barker and Iantaffi, 2019).

In such a short piece of writing, we can only offer a brief sense of these things, but hopefully it will give you some useful invitations to reflect on where your experiences and opinions align with—and differ from—ours, if these questions are interesting to you too.

## Plurality and disability

Our understanding of disability aligns with disability justice and neuroqueer feminist frameworks, both of which endeavor to escape the binary of medical vs. social models of disability (Iantaffi, 2022). Medical models tend to locate disability in the individual person as a form of impairment or deviation from a supposedly healthy norm. Social models locate disability in the society that is built to enable some kinds of—assumed normal—bodyminds, and, in doing so, disables others. For example, we're personally disabled by situations where there is a lot of stimulation—in relation to our autism—and in situations where we're expected to keep going for a long time—in relation to our fatigue. We wouldn't be disabled if such situations accommodated the needs of neurodivergent bodyminds and bodyminds with the levels of energy that ours (sometimes) has.

Neuroqueer feminist and disability justice frameworks point out that purely social models risk denying the lived realities of disability for many people. For example, Merri Lisa Johnson (2021) examines the feminist argument that medical models of borderline personality disorder (BPD) pathologize women who don't fit ideals of femininity. She points out that, while helpful in some ways, such arguments risk erasing the very real suffering that many borderline people experience. They also risk dishonoring those who want to do something to address their suffering at the level of their individual bodymind as well as—or instead of—at the level of the collective. We need approaches that center the lived experience of those most impacted (Berne *et al.*, 2018) and which hold both the individual *and* the social, the personal *and* the political (Iantaffi, 2022).

How does this relate to plurality? For a long time, the only available understanding of plurality available in dominant culture, in countries like the UK and US, was that of multiple personality disorder (MPD; now called dissociative identity disorder, DID). MPD was a cousin diagnosis to BPD, which was similarly often regarded as one of the most severe and intractable "psychiatric disorders." It also carried the additional stigma of being regarded—by many psychologists—as being fabricated or made up. Popular representations of MPD were almost always of extreme "madness" and/or "badness," notably in thrillers where multiples were depicted as having selves who were violently homicidal (see Barker, 2020).

Alongside this understanding of plurality, and becoming more accepted in recent years, were a set of approaches which argue that everyone is plural. Such approaches suggest that the "singular self myth" or "monomind" perspective is a form of cultural normativity, and that accepting your plurality and learning how to relate between all your selves is actually a sign of good health for everybody. Such an approach is taken by Internal Family Systems (Schwartz, 2021) and other less well-known plural perspectives (see Fadiman and Gruber, 2020 for an overview), as well as in 12-step recovery programs which emphasize reparenting and inner child work (e.g. ACA, 2021). Please check out our writing on plurality listed at the end of this chapter if you're interested in exploring some of these ideas further.

While psychiatric understandings of DID can erase those whose plurality is a positive or neutral experience, there's a risk that "healthy plurality" understandings can erase the traumatic roots of some manifestations of plurality, and the very real pain that some plural folks experience. Also, some of these "healthy plurality" understandings can feel rather metaphorical in their depiction of parts of the self, rather than capturing vivid lived experiences of multiplicity.

A binary of pathological versus healthy plurality has also shown up in plural communities—for example, in the "genic" disputes that began in some online communities around a decade ago (Lee, 2020). There were divisions between "trau-magenic" plurals who experienced their plurality as rooted in trauma—including those who identified with DID—and "endogenic" plurals who didn't. Sometimes a real/fake binary has been imposed on the trauma/endo binary, with those in one, or other, category being presented as "really" plural or as faking it. Public accusations of faking plurality have become more prevalent—from outside and within communities—now that systems are sharing their plural selves via video on platforms like TikTok (Lucas, 2021).

Our own experience is that our plurality is a beautiful thing and a vital part of our therapeutic and spiritual path. It has brought us towards a far more honest, loving, compassionate way of relating with ourselves—and others—than we ever had before we recognized our plurality and embraced all of us fully. At the same time, we recognize that the way our plurality *manifested*—throughout our life and in recent years when we finally recognized it fully—has been deeply impacted by trauma. We personally feel that it was the *disowning* of certain selves—due to cultural and developmental trauma—that was traumatic. It was doing that which meant we went through several periods in our life severely impacted by symptoms of post-traumatic stress (PTS; Barker, 2023a). So we take the *both/ and* approach to plurality: a radically non-pathologizing view of plurality, alongside a trauma-informed perspective on how plurality—and singularity—can manifest.

Sadly, like many people, our plural journey has been haunted by all the stigmatizing, erasing and hierarchical views of plurality that continue to dominate. We suspect that the last five years would have been much easier if some of us hadn't had to keep confronting internalized perspectives that our plurality wasn't "real," or that it meant that we were deeply flawed or broken in the ways implied by both DID and BPD psychiatric criteria. While we were massively lucky to find a plural-affirmative therapist and some friends who shared our perspectives, we also felt people distance themselves from us when we talked about our plurality. Some also expressed ambivalence because they related with it themselves but feared what going towards that might mean. We certainly fear that our writing about plurality may be used to attack or dismiss us, especially in the current climate of intense questioning of the legitimacy of other marginalized experiences such as trans and non-binary.

We wonder how many plural folk have similarly gone through inner pain and turmoil, and lost close relationships, during their journeys. Also how many more currently singular-expressing people could benefit hugely from opening to plurality, but fear doing so due to stigma and/or from worry that they may not be "plural enough" for some understandings of plurality.

Given all of this, we can certainly say that those who openly express their plurality are disabled in our current context. Plurality is also deeply interconnected with other forms of disability. For us, this includes our autism, our PTS, the chronic fatigue, pain and dizziness we often experience (related to the lingering impact of a long virus and to menopause), and experiences of deafness through our life.

To give just a few examples of these interconnections, the selves who we most disowned and severed from were those we had to hide as a marginalized autistic person (Price, 2022). Our periods of PTS related to those selves having carried trauma for so long, and eclipsing us with their unbearable feelings when life became overwhelming (Fisher, 2019). Some of the impossible tensions within our traumatized selves show up as somatic pain, fatigue and dizziness. Also, going through menopause seemed to connect one of our most traumatized selves to the violent experiences she had around menarche 40 years ago. For us, deafness also interconnected with our autism (struggling to hear in noisy environments), with physical sickness (frequent viruses and infections causing intense pain and deafness when we were young, and in recent years) and with trauma (being bullied for not being able to hear, and attempting to mask both the deafness and the bullying).

Rather than trying to tease apart different forms of disability (e.g. cognitive, psychiatric, physical, sensory), we find it useful to open to the plurality of ways we are (each) disabled, to the complex—often unknowable—interconnections between them and to what they open up—and close down—for us.

## Plurality and trans

Turning to trans, we take a broad, encompassing understanding of trans which includes those who *transition* from one sex/gender to another, those who *transform* themselves in ways to align more with the sex/gender they experience themselves as being, those who *transgress* normative ways of understanding or expressing sex/gender and more.

As with plurality and disability, we want to hold a wide enough umbrella of trans to encompass the experiences of all trans people, including those who align with more conventional or radical narratives. Indeed, we would go so far as to trouble the cis/trans binary (Iantaffi and Barker, 2017), given that many people who don't identify as trans experience gender transitions during their lives and/or do not feel congruent with the version of masculinity or femininity that they were expected to conform to at birth.

Any understanding of trans has to acknowledge that people have identified and expressed their genders in radically different ways across time and place (Heyam, 2022). Also, as with plurality and disability, it needs to be critical of any sense of "one true way" of being trans, or "trans enough" hierarchies. At the same time, we have to recognize that we operate within a dominant culture which is highly ciscentric and violently transphobic, and where certain trans narratives are often required for accessing support and interventions.

Personally, our plural journey was deeply interwoven with our trans journey. We began identifying as non-binary, and sought out trans care, because of an increasing awareness of one—and then more—masculine selves (having been assigned female at birth). Lacking a plural framework, we initially wondered if we—as an individual self—was "really" transmasculine, or somewhere between masculine and feminine. After top surgery, and then taking testosterone, our experience of our masculine selves became a lot more vivid. At the same time, we felt a continued strong sense of one or more feminine selves who didn't want—or need—to step back, or disappear, in order for the masculine selves to exist. As we moved through our period of deep plural work, it gradually became clear that we had three—then two—feminine selves, three—then two—masculine selves and one non-binary self (Barker, 2022, 2023a).

While by no means all trans people identify—or experience themselves—as plural, it could be argued that all plurals are trans under an encompassing definition of the term. Many plurals have selves of different genders and/or non-gendered beings in their systems. Some plurals may have a sense that those selves who are in the gender they were assigned at birth are cis, and those who aren't are trans. Others—like us—might experience all of their selves as trans, without a clear sense of an original gender that might have been deviated from or aligned with. Even those whose selves are all of the same gender could also be seen as multiply gendered, as they manifest different forms of, say, masculinity or femininity in their different selves. Of course, whether or not a person or system *identifies* as trans is up to them, and depends on their meaning of trans.

Some plurals may express their genders very differently in different selves (clothes, speech, bodily movement, etc.). Others may know the difference internally but feel they have to mask it with a consistent appearance. Some, like us, fall between these poles, as we're all relatively comfortable with the same wardrobe, but we do speak and move differently, particularly when around others who embrace our plurality. Also, as with age and other characteristics, the gender of each self can shift over time or manifest in different ways at different times.

However, there are sadly significant risks both for plurals who want to access trans care and for trans people who want to move towards exploring plurality. One concern we have is that trans people who are open about plurality in gender care settings could be pathologized as DID (according to standard psychiatric models), whether or not they identify this way. As with neuro-divergence, mental health issues and disabilities more broadly, this could mean that practitioners would be more skeptical of the reality of their transness and/or more reluctant to give them access to services (Howitt, 2022). Our other concern is that, in the current climate, anti-trans movements could use the existence of plurality as another reason to question the reality of trans. They might even argue that everyone should embrace plurality *instead* of accessing affirming hormones and surgeries. While there are plural trans people—and singular trans people—who feel no need for bodily alteration, many find such changes to be essential. For example, we would struggle hugely to feel all of our selves in this body if it had a very vivid cultural marker of gender such as breasts or a permanent penis.

When we were invited to give a talk to gender practitioners about plurality, we made these notes of caution, and also presented a number of ways in which plural understandings might be useful for trans people who haven't come across them before. For example, in addition to opening up the possibility of having differently gendered selves, plurality can enable us to welcome child selves who never got to experience themselves in the gender that they felt aligned with back when they were young (see Roche, 2020). Plurality can enable us to honor masking selves who kept us safe before we were able to express our transness, or to find compassion for critical/rejecting selves who have painfully internalized transphobic messages. Plurality can help us to recognize the validity of drag personas or aspects of us who come out in contexts like sex or play. Plurality can help us to access, or manifest, parental, elder or witnessing selves who may draw on archetypes such as the compassionate mother, wise one or warrior.

In a dominant culture as heavily—and rigidly—gendered as ours, it could be argued that most people are likely to have disowned aspects of themselves related to the gender they weren't assigned at birth. Authors like Butler (2002) have argued that they may well experience a sense of loss or melancholia about this. This may be a reason behind the combined envy and hatred inherent in some forms of transphobia (Barker, 2023b). Given this, we could suggest that an exploration of plural gender possibilities—in some form—might be helpful for everyone (see Barker and Iantaffi, 2019).

## Conclusions

To conclude, here are some thoughts towards a trans-affirmative, disability justice-inspired framework for plurality, applying Berne et al.'s (2018) key disability justice principles. Here we highlight both how plurals are disabled and constrained in the current cultural context *and* the enabling and expansive potentials of plurality. Here we're inspired by Travis Alabanza (2022) who asks what everyone might learn from trans people, viewing us as a gift rather than any kind of problem to be fixed.

- **Intersectionality:** Plurality, disability and trans are complexly interconnected. Personal experiences of plurality are inextricably embedded in the systems and structures we're part of, and our plurality intersects with our experience in relation to other systems of power and oppression (gender, race, class, other disabilities, etc.).

- **Leadership of those most impacted:** We need to trust people's lived experience of themselves *and* encompass all experiences and understandings of plurality. We need to move away from oppressive binaries and hierarchies so that everyone who wants to can be open about plurality with themselves and others, and find support and community.

- **Anti-capitalist politics:** The capitalistic, colonialist, white supremacist ideal of a singular, successful, consistent, rational, agentic self disables many people who can't, or won't, conform to this. It also contributes to many of the crises and injustices that currently face us (see Akómoláfé, 2021). This includes disabling plurals and denying all those who might find plural understandings and practices helpful the possibility of moving towards them.

- **Collective access:** There are many diverse, valid ways of understanding, identifying and expressing plurality which may be complementary and/or contradictory, and which require diverse forms of access intimacy (Mingus, 2017).

- **Recognizing wholeness:** Plurals are inherently worthy, essential and whole *and* many carry trauma in some of their selves, often as a result of disconnecting from—or disowning—them for so long. We can take an affirmative, non-pathologizing view of plurality while also acknowledging the reality—and impact—of cultural and developmental trauma on all of us, including gendered forms of trauma (Iantaffi, 2020). We can also recognize that each self *within* each system is inherently valuable, vital and whole, however much they have been shaped by trauma.

- **Cross-disability solidarity:** Plural experiences of learning to live and relate well within internal systems of similarity *and* difference may have much to offer in terms of collectivity and solidarity in communities (see Bevensee, 2018).

- **Cross-movement organizing:** Plurals may have a particularly deep knowing of Audre Lorde's concept that no one is free until we're all free (Lorde, 1997). Many plural paths involve liberating all of our selves and a vivid sense of how our system isn't free until all within it have been liberated. We may also have a particular clarity of the ways in which we are all systems embedded within—and infused by—wider systems (see Bartlett, n.d.).

- **Collective liberation:** This experience of liberating selves in the inner system may have much to offer movements towards collective liberation.

# References

ACA (2021). *The Loving Parent Guidebook.* Signal Hill, CA: ACA WSO.

Akómoláfé, B. (2021). 'You are not a "self."' Bayoakomolafe.net, August 3, 2021. Available from: https://bayoakomolafe.net/post/you-are-not-a-self

Alabanza, T. (2022). *None of the Above.* Edinburgh: Canongate Books.

Barker, M.-J. (2020). 'Plural Selves, Queer, and Comics.' *Journal of Graphic Novels and Comics, 11,* 4, 463–474.

Barker, M.-J. (2022). 'Plural Selves 2.' Rewriting the Rules. Available from: www.rewriting-the-rules.com/zines/#1666773481636-89244c23-4a43

Barker, M.-J. (2023a). 'Triangles (and Circles) of Selves.' Rewriting the Rules. Available from: www.rewriting-the-rules.com/zines/#1699530192652-bd07157b-78f8

Barker, M.-J. (2023b). 'The Gender Wars and Difficult Conversations about Trans.' In R. Ryan-Flood, I. Crowhurst and L. James-Hawkins (Eds) *Difficult Conversations: A Feminist Dialogue*. London: Routledge.

Barker, M.-J. and Iantaffi, A. (2019). *Life Isn't Binary*. London: Jessica Kingsley Publishers.

Bartlett, R.D. (n.d.). 'Five Scales of Microsolidarity.' Microsolidarity. Available from: www.microsolidarity.cc/essays/five-scales-of-microsolidarity

Berne, P., Morales, A.L., Langstaff, D. and Invalid, S. (2018). 'Ten principles of disability justice.' *WSQ: Women's Studies Quarterly*, 46, 1, 227–230.

Bevensee, E. (2018). 'Widening the Bridges: Beyond Consent and Autonomy.' Emotional Anarchism, July 28, 2018. Available from: https://c4ss.org/content/50557

Butler, J. (2002). *Gender Trouble*. London: Routledge.

Fadiman, J. and Gruber, J. (2020). *Your Symphony of Selves*. Paris, ME: Park Street Press.

Fisher, J. (2019). *Healing the Fragmented Selves of Trauma Survivors*. New York, NY: Routledge.

Heyam, K. (2022). *Before We Were Trans*. London: Basic Books.

Howitt, H. (2022). 'How we fuck and unfuck the world.' YouTube. Available from: www.youtube.com/watch?v=gfEBhfhePdk

Iantaffi, A. (2020). *Gender Trauma*. London: Jessica Kingsley Publishers.

Iantaffi, A. (2022). 'Disability and CNM Relationships.' In M.D. Vaughan and T.R. Burnes (Eds) *The Handbook of Consensual Non-Monogamy Affirming Mental Health Practice*. Lanham, MD: Rowman and Littlefield.

Iantaffi, A. and Barker, M.-J. (2017). *How to Understand Your Gender*. London: Jessica Kingsley Publishers.

Johnson, M.L. (2021). 'Neuroqueer feminism: Turning with tenderness toward borderline personality disorder.' *Signs: Journal of Women in Culture and Society*, 46, 3, 635–662.

LB_Lee (2020). 'Quick 'n' dirty plural history, part 4.' August 31, 2020. Available from: https://lb-lee.dreamwidth.org/1129216.html

Lorde, A. (1997). 'The uses of anger.' *WSQ: Women's Studies Quarterly*, 25, 1/2, 278–285.

Lucas, J. (2021). 'Inside TikTok's booming dissociative identity disorder community.' Input, July 6, 2021. Available from: www.inverse.com/input/culture/dissociative-identity-disorder-did-tiktok-influencers-multiple-personalities

Mingus, M. (2017). 'Access intimacy, interdependence, and disability justice.' Leaving Evidence, April 12, 2017. Available from: https://leavingevidence.wordpress.com/2017/04/12/access-intimacy-interdependence-and-disability-justice

Price, D. (2022). *Unmasking Autism: Discovering the New Faces of Neurodiversity*. Chatsworth, CA: Harmony.

Roche, J. (2020). *Gender Explorers*. London: Jessica Kingsley Publishers.

Schwartz, R. (2021). *No Bad Parts*. Louisville, CO: Sounds True.

For our other writing on plurality, and for links to further resources, check out our Plural Selves zines (www.rewriting-the-rules.com/zines), and our Plurality free books (www.rewriting-the-rules.com/plural-work).

# Embodying (in)valid identities: balancing betwixt and between being "enough"

SHANNA KATZ KATTARI, PHD, MED, CSE

School of Social Work and Department of Women's and Gender Studies, University of Michigan

I remember when the book *Balancing on the Mechitza: Transgender in Jewish Community* made its way into my orbit (Dzmura, 2014); the visual image that the title conjured immediately etched itself into my brain. The *mechitza* is the divider in Orthodox Jewish spaces that separates the men and boys from the women and girls in Temple—and not in a transgender-inclusive way. This book captures the challenges of embodying a gender outside of the strict men/women binary that is upheld in many more traditional Jewish spaces. Inspired by this divider visual, an idea for this essay came to me. Visualize, however you will, a white, middle-class, disabled, neurodivergent, chronically ill, Jewitchy,[1]

---

1   Jewish by heritage, ethnicity, and some practice; witchy by choice and practice.

queer, fat, nonbinary femme, with curly red hair, sparkly cats' eyeglasses, a smattering of tattoos, and a rainbow-studded mobility cane, perched atop a mechitza, or a garden wall, or a tightrope, struggling to balance as they navigate betwixt and between identity groups. That is often what I feel like as I delve through, around, over, in, and out of identities that are often challenged as made up, too much, or not real, or whether they are even "enough" to have their own labels. Whether I am even "enough" to have these labels as my own. This pushback comes not only from external forces; I also inundate myself with these trepidations on a repeated loop. I am someone who is constantly questioning whether I truly am who I say I am, or whether I am actually a skilled charlatan who has managed to deceive pretty much everyone I know (thanks brain and your intrusive thoughts!). The process of exploring, claiming, and affirming identities is such a convoluted one. Does the imposter syndrome ever stop?

Living in the gray is both so easy for me when I am able to just be authentically who I am and also really challenging when I come up against society's constant gatekeeping of so many identities, of all the pieces of who I am. The thoughts twist in my brain, sometimes loudly, sometimes more muted, but they are always, always, always there. Thoughts like:

> Perhaps I am not nonbinary enough to own that term—am I just doing this for attention? Maybe I really am not disabled enough to claim that language—so many people experience ableism in much more explicit ways.

And don't even get me started on the challenges of being autistic in a world that still assumes all autists are cis het white boys who are good with numbers and bad with social skills. The intrusive thoughts mentioned here often play into the issues of living situated firmly in the in-between; I am neither the number-smart autistic trope, nor am I brilliant in an arts-based way, following the other popular autistic stereotype. Does that mean I'm making that all up? Does that mean I am not brilliant in my own way?[2] How hard it is to own and embody your own identities when you yourself are one of your toughest and meanest critics about your own validity, loudly echoing society's critiques.

Despite all of the struggle, there is still such beauty in knowing who you are. In finding the words that slide over you and perfectly click. The labels that fill every nook and cranny, eliminating the void of being unknown to yourself. When we find ourselves, in language and in community, it feels like coming home.

## Finding home/coming home

### *"What the fuck even is a nonbinary femme?"*

I asked myself this before anyone else ever did, though, rest assured, I still get asked this often. People struggle with gray, overlap, multiplicities, or whatever you prefer to call the space that exists outside of the either/or binaries that our society aggressively pushes us towards, and shames us for resisting if we opt out of neatly placed lines and boxes. I struggled with balancing the part of me that loves femme-ness, the camp of glitter and dresses and fun colored lipstick, with the part of me for whom the word "woman" feels like a coat that just doesn't fit, the part that just never felt like "one of the girls."

Often, I am asked why I bother with my nonbinary identity

---

2 Both partners of mine who read this were emphatic in the addition of such a sentence, as they gave incredible pushback on my own self critique that I wasn't smart and artistic and brilliant. Get yourself some wonderful folks on your team who call you and your brain in through such loving ways.

even though I am a femme, because it would be so much "easier" (their words) to either present as the stereotype of nonbinary-ness with shorter hair, Carhartt's, and a flannel button-down, or to stick with my presentation and just accept being (reluctantly) associated with womanhood. This logic reminds me of the question those of us attracted to butches are often asked: if you want someone who looks like a man, why don't you just date a man? The lack of our collective willingness to understand the nuances of gender, of sexuality, of disability, of race, of so many things, is constantly astounding to me.

Autists may be deemed black/white, either/or, absolute thinkers, yet I cannot wrap my head around the idea that I have to choose only one thing, then clear cut pieces of myself that don't fit within the framework, and throw them by the wayside to be left behind. The more that I have tried to explore my gender, and my disability and neurodivergence, the more that I've realized I cannot completely separate each of them. In fact, they overlap with and inform one another in fascinating and sometimes striking ways.

One mechanism through which I've noticed the embodiment of such identities is my style and sense of fashion. What I wear and how I wear it are not necessarily for the gaze of others (though occasionally for a partner, friend, or special occasion). However, how I use my form as a canvas to embody my internal sense of self on display for my external view of self brings me much joy, empowerment, and validation. These are concepts I don't focus on or engage with intentionally, other than just wearing what feels authentic and what brings me joy.

### "You dress like toddler grandma"

Sometimes. The way I present my femme-ness is likened to the beloved illustration/cartoon educator Ms. Frizzle or Penelope Garcia from *Criminal Minds*—I exclusively am found in dresses and skirts, often with plants, animals, celestial bodies, weather patterns, rainbows, or mythical creatures taking front stage. I've sometimes described my style as 1950s Witchy House-wife Unicorn Ms. Frizzle, and I'm told this is a fairly accurate description. While many assume this is correlated exclusively with the femme part of my gender, I believe it also encompasses my neurodivergence (particularly my autism), my disabilities, queerness, and even my fatness.

Until you point it out to them, most people don't realize that *most* pants are more uncomfortable than *most dresses*. As a person with high sensory experiences, and a fat person with a squishy tum, the feeling of something cutting me in half around the waist, whether with tight elastic waistbands or buttons right on my stomach? Ick! When I do wear skirts, they are either super loose, or things like pencil skirts that are meant to be worn higher up, almost above the waist. To me, dresses are like wearing a nightgown out into the world, yet still being seen as professional while doing it.

I should note that I do find many leggings comfortable; however, particularly as a fat person, these are rarely viewed as professional in many spaces. So, while I may wear these as pants with a sassy shirt for physical therapy, or to head over to a partner's house, they are not in my regular rotation. Rather, they are the exception that proves the rule.

Dresses allow me more independence too—on days when I am flaring, or in too much pain, or too exhausted to get dressed completely by myself, dresses can be an easy solution to just toss over my head. When going to the bathroom, using a dress is multitudes easier than pants when you think about energy expenditure. In an adjacent vein, two-piece swimsuits can be much easier to get on and off as a disabled person, yet it is hard to find them as a fat person, once again emphasizing how the overlapping of identities impacts how I show up in the world, even for something as minimal as the type of swimsuit I wear.

My autism and mental health are connected to all of this too—I choose materials that are sensory friendly, for the most part, and necklines that don't activate me by being too close to my throat, but perhaps most importantly, my outfits bring me joy. Wearing a mushroom dress (with matching earrings, of course) connects me to my love of *mycelium* and foraging, even when I have to deal with grading papers. Selecting from between over a dozen of cat-themed dresses can help give me a little endorphin boost, especially on a day filled with ideation. Looking down and seeing octopus tentacles emerging on my skirt, especially to align with my trip to the aquarium, makes me feel gender euphoria and autistic joy all at once. I too sometimes dress predominantly in black, perhaps with black cat or nonbinary-flag-colored challah earrings—this feels like channeling some of Jewitchy-ness while still feeling comfortable in my clothes, and having a dimmer sensory slate to work from.

## Blazing stars in the galaxy

I live in the in-between. I occupy those spaces on the edges of our known identity universe. I see all of my identities as stars in a galaxy or a cosmos, our perception of them constantly shifting as other variables change (Kattari, 2019). This is where my disability lives, where one day I am using a walker and clearly read as disabled, where the next I might be able to give a talk, not even needing the assistance of a cane. Here too is where my neurodivergence is situated, a swirling blend of autism, depression, anxiety, OCD, and ADHD (maybe? Talk about ever-changing perceptions!). My gender is its own galaxy, firmly anchored in time and space, but with the only constant being NONBINARY FEMME and everything else changing fluidly. While these identities are often challenged in inter-personal contexts as made up, not real, not enough, too much, they are who I am. And as I stare at my black sparkly toenails, my vibrant tattoos, my dress featuring a myriad of woodland creatures, and my earrings that declare "No Justice/No Peace," I realize that perhaps I too am made up, not quite real, an ethe-real being who rides the edges of binaries and floats out of boxes. In fact, isn't everything made up? I may constantly need to remind my own brain that I am nonbinary and trans and autistic and femme (and everything) enough, and to those who may feel I am too much, I would invite them to go find less. We all have the opportunity to explore our own galaxies—come take a moment to fly among the stars!

# References

Dzmura, N. (Ed.). (2014). *Balancing on the Mechitza: Transgender in Jewish Community*. Berkeley, CA: North Atlantic Books.

Kattari, S.K. (2019). 'Troubling binaries, boxes, and spectrums: A galactic approach to queerness and crip-ness.' *QED: A Journal in GLBTQ Worldmaking*, 6, 3, 136–142.

# Intersectionalities

JEONG EUN PARK

When I saw the new *Barbie* movie, I was at first super excited by the representation in it. And then I took a minute to really think about the movie. And what I realized was that disability representation was a blink-and-you-miss-it moment. One scene in which there was a Barbie using a wheelchair and another with a prosthetic arm, but that's it. They had their one moment and then were never seen again.

That feels about right. Disability feels a bit like damned if you do and damned if you don't. If you have a physical disability that people can see, then yeah, it's acknowledged (mostly) and you still have to tackle the ableism in this society. And if your disability is so-called invisible (or, at least, not easily identifiable or discernible), then you are ignored and erased and invalidated. After all, is it real if it isn't seen?

I would have loved to have seen the Barbies include the Barbie in the wheelchair when they plotted to distract the Kens. What would be more ironic than having her ask a Ken to help her since she can't help herself? After all, she's in a wheelchair; she couldn't possibly do anything herself or without help from an able-bodied person!

And the Barbie with the prosthetic arm might have something wrong with it and only a Ken could help her fix it.

Because ableism means we need to be fixed whether we asked for it or not.

But no, and as I look around in this ableist world we live in, I realize that my own intersectionality, as a disabled agender Asian person who also is late-diagnosis autistic and neurodiverse in other ways, gives me a unique position in which I battle ableism, saneism, transphobia, queerphobia, and racism, all in this neat little package.

It's exhausting. On my good days, when my body doesn't hurt and my mind is lucid, I still have to be aware of my surroundings as someone who is perceived to be female and Asian. When the Covid pandemic began, and the Asian hate skyrocketed to include physical acts of violence against Asians, I never went out in public by myself for over a year. I received many glares and mutterings, but thankfully I was never physically attacked.

On my not-so-good days, when my body aches and my mind is clouded from pain or I'm dealing with depression and sometimes suicidality and almost always anxiety, when I am masking my autistic traits so I feel safer but am desperate to stim my anxiety to manageable levels, I function from forcing myself to barely able to move.

I shouldn't feel ashamed or embarrassed, but I was raised to work hard and to achieve my goals. No crybabies allowed. But I feel as though I need to just push on through the pain. It is a dangerous thing, though, and even though people may admire my grit, there's a price to pay for it.

Disability activists have talked about not being put on a pedestal, about not being treated as though those people who are achieving their goals and are disabled are super beings, about how the toxic positivity shoved at us is exhausting.

Exhausting seems to be the theme, and I haven't even touched on being part of the trans community and the challenges to be accepted as an agender/nonbinary/genderfluid/

gender!fuck person where even cisgenderism and "passing" and the binary still are ever present.

I have zero interest in catering to the binary or cisgender anything, and although I do often choose to present more femme, I also prefer the fluidity of being. My pronouns do not match how others perceive me, and sometimes I choose to stay closeted because although I can't hide my Asian face, I can hide my gender while I quietly scream inside from dysphoria and rage and hurt.

My body hurts in a lot of ways. I have chronic illnesses and I'm immunocompromised, and if I'm not careful and move in certain ways, I hurt myself. I have medicine that helps me when I get migraines but then keeps me in bed the rest of the day. I have medicine that helps ease the bodily aches, but I have to take it sparingly to avoid worsening my kidney disease.

My nonbinary self doesn't know how to deal with all of this at times. I don't talk about it. This would really be the first time I've truly written about it but, oh gods—I have the feeling my lifespan isn't going to be especially long and I'm hoping to have another 20 years because I absolutely love love LOVE my sons and I want as much time as I can get with them.

What I do know is that I am proud to be who I am, all that intersectionality that makes up me. I've fought hard to get to here, and I fight hard to stay here, despite what my mind tells me at times.

So I create my own story, and I can distract the Kens of this world. I can advocate for my bodily autonomy, disabled or not, I can claim whatever gender speaks to me, and my gender expression is mine to own. This intersectionality that is ever present for me allows me to show there is so much more to me than being disabled and agender. The world might see those two at the exclusion of everything else but I and the ones who L/love me know there is so much more to who I am.

# I can't keep meeting me like this

## Society Postponing Our Identities Rather Than Embracing Complexity

COLTAN J. SCHOENIKE

A well-trodden notion I've become familiar with as a queer and trans person is how the process of "coming out" isn't a singular event. I've been told, as well as told others countless times, that as we go throughout our lives, we will constantly meet and interact with new people and thus must come out again and again. Despite the implied exhaustion from having to re-disclose into perpetuity, there can be some consolation when the identity you are disclosing is at least the same one each time. This may be the case for many people, and it also felt that way for me earlier in my life. In recent years, my experience and process of self-identity hasn't been so simple.

As I've reflected on my own history and timeline of self-identity and the trajectory which ultimately led me to my present sense of queer, trans, nonbinary, neurodivergent, and disabled self, I find myself wondering how this evolution has come to be. Why so many changes? It's important to note this is not intending to infer that there is anything wrong with experiencing fluidity in one's identities and experiences. Fluidity is a beautiful component of the diversity of humanity. The fluctuation I speak of in my own life is less about things growing and evolving as time passes; rather, these many shifts and changes all feel like things that were there the whole time but had been obscured from me or I was not given the information to access them. It feels as if I'm being dealt a hand of cards, but the dealer is only handing me one card at a time, *very* slowly, while the game continues around me and I'm having to guess what cards I might get as I place my bets. As I finally get dealt another card after what feels like years later (and can be literal years when you move back outside the metaphor), I find myself thinking, "Well, it would have been nice to know that was the card in my hand all this time I've been playing." Of course, I'm probably still waiting on at least two or three more cards I haven't gotten yet. And still I'm expected to keep playing.

In many of the experiences I've had of this phenomenon, whether it's my queerness, gender identity, expression, neurodivergence, or ability, I find that a common cause of these staggered self-discoveries is the fact that many of my own experiences with them are nuanced, outside of binary or stereotype, and don't match the traditionally dominant story society has been told about them. These narratives like to keep things simple and rely on them appearing or existing in only one particular way. With that expectation in place, one whose experiences don't match those neat and tidy descriptions is forced to unlearn those stories and challenge those restrictive and confining criteria of acceptability before they are at all able to engage in their own self-discovery and exploration with those identities and lived experiences. For me, this has manifested as constantly having to re-meet myself, or encounter those new (to me) aspects of my experience that had been there the whole time but were just not yet accessible to me.

My first example of this would be around my gender and sexuality, both of which fall outside of the traditional binary options imposed upon them. I knew early on in my life as someone assigned male at birth that I was not entirely heterosexual, but I did not have the language until later in my adolescence to understand the countless opportunities that existed beyond the either/or of straight or gay. My gender was in a similar situation, where even the remote possibility of identity beyond man or woman was not available to me until college when I was able to receive the language to now better understand a pain and longing for something different that was there my entire life, even if I couldn't describe it until now. Even after gaining language with which to explore my identity, dominant narratives of transness both from outside and within the community led to the constant questioning: "Am I trans enough?" The "enough" is key here, and I think it is a common thread throughout many of these experiences. The self-doubts enforced by society's aversion to nuanced stories of human diversity only exacerbate the problems. Sure, the dealer is handing my card to me super slowly, but it doesn't help when the game also has me questioning: "Is that actually my card or were you meant to hand that to someone else? If I take this card, is this compromising someone else's hand?" Even now, I find myself having intrusive doubts as I explore these thoughts. Am I "disabled enough" to be writing this, and am I taking this away from someone else?

There are countless insidious ways that society's aversion to nuance and dependence on oversimplified narratives cause problems. I mentioned previously how I could not access language or understanding around gender until in college, and I similarly was not able to understand my own experiences of sexual violence as a teen without that education either. One truly cannot describe the pain of suddenly realizing years later that you were sexually assaulted by an intimate partner, and *that* was why you felt so off and uncomfortable, crying as you drove home. There is a feeling of deep grief in finding this out years later and wondering to yourself what the healing journey could have looked like had you truly understood what had happened right then and there. Exacerbating this pain is also the doubt, inserting itself into you like stinging knives as it whispers, "If you couldn't tell what it was at the time, could it have been all that bad? Aren't you just making this up?"

Even outside of truly traumatic and tragic circumstances, there is a grief that comes as a consequence of society's oversimplification. When I was first diagnosed with ADHD, I was 24 and in my master's program training to be a therapist. One thing I do look back at as one spot of cosmic humor among the grief is that I was in my diagnosis class at the time. The instructor and one of the most significant mentors in my professional journey noted that many of us will have the experience in the class where we are reading the various mental health diagnoses, and each of us will come to the conclusion that we have many of them, despite that likely not being true. I laugh as I think about the fact that I did, after all, come out of that semester with a new diagnosis, somehow feeling a dark sense of achievement at doing the impossible. Because of that class, I also came to realize not only that I should explore that possible diagnosis but why it was not considered previously. Consistent with society's love for the overly simplified, binary, and stereotypical, many mental health and neurodivergent diagnoses have historically been very heavily influenced by gender in how they are diagnosed, what are considered to be criteria, and if a person even gets diagnosed at all. Looking at the signs throughout my own life of "How on earth did no one notice this?" the way my ADHD manifested was much more consistent with the stereotypical presentations of ADHD in girls than in boys. Feeding two birds with one hand, this explained how I went under the radar for so long as well as adding a little bit of weird validation and cosmic humor to my now identifying as a transfeminine person. The validation and humor pieces aside, there is still that grief that is there, wondering what life would have looked like for me all those years beforehand, having definitely struggled immensely through high school and my undergraduate degree, relying heavily on the grace and kindness of countless professors, as well as many, *many* extensions.

Even now, I find myself in the throes of having to renegotiate my sense of self and identity, as well as how I navigate the world. In recent years, I've come to be more aware of Ehlers-Danlos and other hypermobility and connective tissue conditions. As I write this, I'm not in the camp of "officially diagnosed." Rather, I'm finding myself in a space of it being highly suspected and more likely than not as I hope to work toward maybe exploring it more officially. Obviously, such a venture is easier said than done in our current healthcare system (at least here in the United States). In the meantime, I just have to work with the "more likely than not" and go by the assumption that it's probably the case, so I can get started on figuring out what I need to do to accommodate myself and my needs as a disabled person in a multitude of ways and with varying degrees of confirmation. And even then, there's that "enough" again. If it's not formally diagnosed, am I disabled enough? Can I name my lived experience as valid?

All this is to say, this process is exhausting. On top of the countless individual griefs I have for each of these parts of myself I've had to gradually discover one after the other, and what could have been had I known earlier, there's also the over-all grief for this system that has made it this way. Further than grief, there's anger and resentment. I feel as though I and others are being punished for society's aversion to nuance, and the refusal to do anything other than rely on oversimplification and stereotypes. It is already an arduous and complex process to know oneself, but it is all the more painful when you are instructed time and time again to stop and start over repeatedly. Nonetheless, I know the age-old adage: the best time to plant a tree is 20 years ago, but the second best time to plant a tree is today. I will not resign myself to deciding there's a point of being "too late" to explore a part of myself, and I hope others do not resign themselves either. I hope that there is also the systemic work being done to embrace nuance and recognize the beautiful diversity of human experiences. I hope society will allow us to be enough, in whatever multitude of ways. If we challenge the rules and stories that force a delay in our experiences of self-discovery around things that have always been there, we will be able to make room for organic exploration of who we want to be, and getting what we need to support that growth. Is that so much to ask?

# Beast of burden

## SILAS BOURNS

*What good is a beast of burden once it has served its purpose?*

*If it can no longer provide its role of service, what can it become?*

*A tanned hide. A piece of meat. An exhausted corpse.*

*What good is a girl that has served its purpose?*

*When he injects himself using shaky
hands that threaten to claw,*

*what can he become?*

*A monster of two kinds. A useless animal. An exhausted corpse.*

*If my horns grow longer and my teeth sharper,*

*will it matter when I tear into flesh if it ruins my own?*

*Personhood is conditional; monstrosity is
a bed you sleep in for eternity.*

# Loving with defiance: breaking a binary, not a b1n0ry

KITTY LU BEAR

"Para todos todo, para nosotros nada."—EZLN[1]

On Guy Fawkes Day, in the year of the High Priestess, a nebula was born from the dust. A gust of wind blew 378 days later and on November 17, 1983 in eastern Chiapas, the Zapatista Army of National Liberation was founded (EZLN). Firmly planted, a radical rooting, enveloped by the weird knowings to fruit.

A whole with three times ten plus six[2], rounded to swallow, becomes legendary math.

## Part 1

I am trans and disabled.

Small words for big experiences—what could be better than to bend time and space? Let's try a new pace.

---

1    Words of resistance from EZLN—"Everything for everyone. Nothing for us." Thank you, **EZLN**.
2    Legendary mathematics from the song "Trust Is Silent But Speaks Loud" from ALL THE DREAMS I EVER HAD. Thank you, **Time** and **AwareNess**.

I am (trans) and (disabled).

I am (trans) because I am (disabled) and I am (disabled) because I am (trans). Pause your mind for a moment; the multiverse beckons.

I am trans and disabled and multiple and autistic and Mad and chronically sick and and and and I am trans and agender and genderqueer and genderfucked and cosmically gendered, a nebula grieving death as their stars are born, a multidimensional experience of the *we* not the *me*, but I see time and I feel time and I breathe time and I stop time and I am disabled.

It's weird being disabled because your nervous system is dialed to a setting beyond this universe.

It's weird being trans because your identity is fluid, dynamically liberated, like the river to the sea, the oceanic mysteries of the Sargasso Sea.

It seems the eels only know me.

Some things are best left to the unknown. The crows know, the eels know. The mystery lies in what is a blood type, but the identity of ancient stars laying wait as iron, for the next call to sharpen.

Being the flavor of autistic that is nestled in the arms of madness, sleeping peacefully in between the lineages of the weird knowers and the pathologically murdered by systems younger than the moon is a strange existence. Gender slips through my fingers like meteorite showers falling in your peripherals. I am unknown by those who don't need to know in this timeline. I am known by those who can see with their eyes closed.

I am trans and disabled.

I am more than *me*, the cosmic *we* caught lovingly in a body mapped to the constellations written from a timeline yet to happen. Who can unlock the paradox of me when we haven't made the key yet?

Time keeps all secrets in the mirrors of souls. It's the real reason I can't look you in the eye.

Time keeps all secrets in the treetops with the crows. It's the real reason I walk on my toes.

Don't believe what the books say; this experience is beyond words written. I use they/them pronouns because I am more than just the one pronoun. I use they/them pronouns because I am more than just one person.

I use they/them pronouns because I am plural, never singular.

I use they/them pronouns because it is easier for you to call *me* unknown than to see us as a *we* known.

I use they/them pronouns and still you can only see this body as it fits to your limitations. Don't cage me just because you locked your own cuffs.

The only thing we have to lose is our chains. I know it is our duty to win.[3] I use they/them pronouns.

I am trans and disabled.

## Part 2

I am trans and disabled.

I am (one thing) and (another thing).

I am (this ~~complicated~~ complex thing).

I am two things, a single thing that is never just one, so sometimes it's three. Or more. Sometimes never.

I am trans and disabled.

I am (trans) and (disabled).

---

3   Reference to this wisdom from Assata Shakur: "It is our duty to fight for our freedom. It is our duty to win. We must love each other and support each other. We have nothing to lose but our chains." Thank you, **Assata**.

Covered in parentheses, hidden in the spaces invisible to the i's.

We speak in numbers. Patterns, repetition and its vibrant silence when gone. Our gender is prime, but not just any prime. Though it could be conceived that prime numbers are the genderfuckery of numeracy. Prime numbers, whose only existence is aptly reflected by the neo one, a reflective surface that defies logical resistance and exists in complement to the none (but not empty), to the nonnegative wheel that breaks into undefined (the real binory). Prime numbers whose only factors are itself and the neo one, the mirror. Prime numbers who can only reflect upon themselves because no other numbers can be amplified to be them. No other numbers can multiply, combine, connect, collect, and become who they are. Our gender is prime, the most prime. If the most prime prime could exist, we would be it.

[A prime number is a whole number whose only two factors are 1 and itself. Factors are numbers that you can multiply together to get another number.]

However, not all prime numbers are the same. Almost all prime numbers are odd, a consideration that to be prime is to be a misfit, an outlier, an odd one.

Yet not all odd numbers are prime. The one direction fallacy of squares and rectangles is a pervasive metric throughout most of mathematics. However, there is one prime number that breaks the minds of mathematics, bends the nuances of numeracy, blurs orthogonal time at its best.

The number 2.[4] I know, I know.

2. A supposed binary.

---

4   I despaired the number 2 most of my life because of ordinal linguistic personification synesthesia. Another timeline intersected and my course was redirected, repaired. Thank you, **annabelle**.

(fuck a binary, not the b1n0ry)

Still, the number 2 may be the most prime of all primes because it is the only even prime number.

The only one.

A numerical hapax legomenon. A curious mathematical rollercoaster, a first of many firsts, to not be considered cardinally a first.

The only one that is not the one.

2 is curious, not only in it being the only even prime number to exist but it transgresses the cis-temic expectation that math follows a generative pattern. To add is to increase.

To multiply is to increase more than addition.

To be exponential is far greater than any multiplication.

(And just for fun, to be a factorial is a house party of numerical proportions.) Yet 2 defies them all.

2 chooses to love with defiance.[5] 2 chooses to not only be queer and be here, to not only be gay and do crime, but to be trans and burn empires down. To break math into genderfucked chaos, where existence is not defined by operations, where loving yourself, becoming more yourself, is the same no matter what external conditions are present.

2 chooses to love with defiance.

$2 + 2 = 4$

$2 \times 2 = 4$

$2^2 = 4$

When 2 is transformed, it becomes 4. The smallest composite number, a multiplicity standing in cosmic quantum form, defiant in love.

The 4. The four. The four turtles. The four sides of a kite,

---

5   Reference to words from *The Zapatistas' Dignified Rage: Final Public Speeches of Subcommander Marcos.* Thank you, (former) **Subcommander Marcos**.

white with a long tail.[6] The four seasons. A year leaping. A tetris, defying configurations. The basic states, a cross to square with holy intent. The general specialness of a relative force. The valiant nature of elemental existence, included in the breath of four chambers. The four riders. The four holy cities. A death, a birth. The four truths, noble and known. All time, happening at all times, as the fourth, yet not final, dimension.

When 2 is transformed, it becomes 4, which is 1 from 3. The shortest distance to madness is when *many* become *more*. When chaos becomes radicalized, connected, defiant in love, uplifted by the 2.

The most prime of all primes because it is the only one to never be one, but it will be the one that is always two. Our gender is prime, the most prime.

2. Two. To. Too.
4. Four. For. *Para*.

We speak in numbers, though our most fluent time signatures flow through the waves of irrationality. A rogue entrance into patterns undone by expectation, a presence to the unchanging aspect of unexpected continuous change. A container with no shape, a murmuration of the minds.

We speak in numbers and our mind is an irrational number, extending in all directions. Our disintegration, our dismissal, our disability falls into the spacetime that breaks logic, breaks down a ratio of divisibility.

We are indivisible, a ratio from another cosmos unable to split apart by the confines of singularity. Our mind math is not nice, nor pleasant, and the patterns that erupt will never repeat.

The real transcendence against systems of oppression, the spine of sanism, is to be unmeasurable by the metrics of sanity.

---

6   You are remembered, **Refaat Alareer**. Thank you, **beloved**.

Measured against all standards, we stand hard in the space that an outlier disabled is a point repaired by despair.

To be undone is to refuse to be unspun, unwoven at the root.

I am not a pretty square root, more akin to a tornado that pulls lava from the earth. Our mind math is not nice, nor does it take any shit. Nothing about us without us because we are indivisible, unable to be grouped and quantified in piles that can be compartmentalized, shuffled, and placed along shelves to sell to the highest bidder. Our mind is an irrational number, siblings to $\pi$ and $e$ and $\gamma$ and imagined in the minds of polymaths who discovered many but refused notoriety for all.

Our only truly disabling factor to our innate ability is that you can't figure us out. Just because you can't quantify us does not mean we are resolved from quality.

Grateful to be absolved by who you think we should be, who you think we could be, who you think we need to be. An absolute value that requires no notation, at least not by your hand, that is.

Our mind math is unfounded by problems solved, existing only in the questions lingering with marks that twist to the stars, like a piece of pi(e) that never ends because our tale is untold, a tail waiting in our wings.

A chimerical structure that equals 2, when faces are connected to intersecting points, separated from the lines that divide, dissolving to what is known to be genderfucked.[7] Or mindfucked. Our mind math is fucked, but check our proofs, each variable accounted for in some timeline of infinite possibilities.

A polyhedra of poly-hydras breathing fire, many heads mean many tales untold. We speak in numbers and our mind is an irrational number. All of them, plus neo one minus

---

7 Euler's infinite polyhedra formula: Vertices + Faces − Edges = 2. Thank you, **Leonhard.**

twice the difference, found between emptiness and complex anti-singularity.

Not all infinities are equal, not all i's are meant to see all, but all eyes know a sea when it claims clams clamor courageously.

I am complex, a numerical mystery fit into the spaces between what is known and what is questioned.

My mind is an irrational number, captured by your limited scribbles. A jam-bearing cosmic fruit, a solution to an unwritten inequality.

We speak in numbers, a language subjective to context, an objective that is always political.

I am trans and disabled.

## Part 3

I am trans and disabled.

I am (not) trans (enough) and (not) disabled (enough). I am (not trans enough and not disabled enough).

I am ( ).

I am the empty set, to forever be compared into fragments of this and that or that and this and never to be whole. An endless hole to be enough would burst stuffed. Ours wave at the sounds of whales, only to be heard in songs.

They say I don't have to, I don't need to, no one needs to know, keep it to yourself. No one wants to know but someone should know.

Some truths are better whispered.

I am (*trans non-binary agender genderqueer genderfabulously fucked by stars in the eyes of skies changing in the faces of bees on flowers*).

I am (*trans resisting gender in all forms but it doesn't matter because you will see this body, this face, this lack of this and this more of that and decide that I am the gender you wish you were).*

**I am** (*trans remembering all the lost ones, the stolen ones, the murdered ones, the ones crying alone in dark corners of cold houses, the ones who love love and love love and love love because they are love).*

**I am** (*trans as in changing at all times, trans as in me, trans as in him, trans as in her, trans as in it, trans as in the void, trans in all dimensions, trans in all timelines).*

**I am** (*trans, not defined by cis standards; stand hard with burning down the cis-tem).*

**I am** (*trans because I claim it).*

**I am** trans enough.

**I am** (*disabled chronically sick chronically ill autistic multiple Mad crip time traveler psycho crazy insane unsane (un)sane undoing sanity).*

**I am** (*disabled with fibromyalgia, IBS, chronic genetic migraines that became a spectrum disorder of intractable migraines and cluster headaches after eight years of psychiatric medical violence that permanently changed the electricity of my mind).*

**I am** (*disabled by meltdowns, sensory overwhelm, sensory underwhelm, inability to read social cues, social views, social language not communicated in body spaces decipherable, self-harm, self-violence, meltdowns, meltdowns, meltdowns).*

**I am** (*disabled by trauma, by panic attacks, by surviving trafficking, by surviving class, by surviving capitalism, by surviving not knowing, by sexual assault, by rape, by violence, by trauma, by pain, by not being believed, by medical neglect, by psychiatric violence, by psychiatric incarceration, by surviving deathwishes embodied and given, by praying to die in my sleep, by praying for death, by obsession, by compulsion, by ticcing, by stimming, by seeing time, by hearing visions, by dreams that come true, by knowing the unknown, by paranoia, by psychosis).*

**I am** (*disabled because of PTSD, C-PTSD,* ~~*Borderline Personality Disorder, Bipolar Disorder I, General Anxiety Disorder,*~~ *Dissociative Identity Disorder, Autism Spectrum Disorder*).

**I am** (*disabled because the DSM screams I am; fuck the DSM, burn it in the fires that will warm our hearts and bodyminds in the mutaineers' thrutopia*[8]).

**I am** (*disabled because I claim it*).

**I am disabled** *enough*.

I am trans and disabled.

---

8   Words belonging to despair repair. Thank you, **carla joy**.

# Self-portrait

MYA SARACHO (@A.LOVEUNLACED)

You can't get through a formal art education without a pile of self-portraits and an intimate knowledge of your own nose. I have sheaves of these self-portraits stuffed in drawers and sketchbooks, and more than a few in trash cans. I haven't drawn my own face since forced at grade-point.

It is a very different face now. It is round with weight gain and steroids, and dotted with injection scars. I have the beginnings of lines around my eyes. But I am still covered in freckles. My nose is the same.

Decades of self-portraits and I have never seen my face as I know it. Decades more of self-portraits and I may never see my face as I know it.

When I cut my hair, my grandmother called me a "modern woman."

I am neither.

When I told my mother I am non-binary, she told me she couldn't see me as a son.

I am not that either.

I am a creature of liminal space. I live in the betweens and swing wildly between the masculine and the feminine, the capable and the incapable, the hungry and the satisfied, the painfully ill and the *ya know, I think today's gonna be alright*. And while I swing, I remember that I am both. Always both.

I am a Gemini, after all.

I am inconsistent. I am lavish parties and last-minute canceled plans. I am a closet of lace and leather. I am *ropa vieja* and, inexplicably, jello salads. I am well-worn suede-bottom shoes and a rubber-tipped cane.

And maybe if I collect each of these truths in self-portraits, I'll see my own face.

So, here I am today. Freckles and hoops. Curls and one of the three standard Minneapolis Queer™ haircuts. Boundless depths and boundless truths, crowned in a migraine.

But I am still covered in freckles. My nose is the same.

# Liminal

ALEX IANTAFFI

Sometimes I wonder what it might be like to not live in the cracks, the in-between spaces that sometimes can be so tight I can hardly breathe, and other times are so vast that I am afraid I might fall to my death if I dare to leap. What would it be like to experience firm belonging in one neat box and rest there for a while? It sounds peaceful but maybe it's constricting. Who knows... *shrug*

This is what I know for sure, like many before me, and that is that change is the only constant. My sense of self has never felt fixed. I wonder if it's because I am hypermobile or a water sign. Lately, I have been wondering about plurality too. What I know, for certain, is that the liminal is where I dwell. If I were a different person, I might ascribe this to a fear of commitment, but I'm quite a loyal and committed person; I am just not comfortable in a single box, and never was.

Long before I read Judith Butler, I already knew that gender was suspect, for example. I think I was around six years old when I realized that my clothes and haircut could "fool" someone into thinking I was a boy, even though I was told I was a girl. If it was as easy as wearing sweatpants, a short haircut and sharing a gender-ambiguous diminutive of my name, surely gender could not be as important as adults around me seem to think. At 17 years old, I called up the aviation division of the military in my country because I wanted to join and be trained as a medic. I was told girls could not join the military, not even as a medic. I asked why. Their answer was deeply unsatisfactory. While I am grateful that I didn't join the military industrial complex, especially since I didn't believe in geopolitical borders and I just wanted a way out of my own home, I am still deeply unsatisfied by their answer.

Eventually, I would go in a very different direction, in another country, and get a whole PhD in what used to be called "Women's Studies" and sometimes still is. I was so eager to understand gender. Before that, I had completed a four-year degree in linguistics in my home country because I wanted to understand communication. A few years after my PhD, I went back into graduate school to complete a Master's in Systemic Psychotherapy because I wanted to make sense of family dynamics. It would be a couple more decades, and moving to yet another country, before I was diagnosed with ADHD with "strong autistic traits" in my very early 50s. It would take five decades of my life for me to understand myself as neurodivergent and reframe many traits I considered to be a moral failure as being part of my AuDHD. It turns out my special interest is people. So many things make sense now. So much grief is still being unearthed within my soul.

I still think gender is suspect, just like I knew at six years old. I just have more words to explain why now. In fact, so many words and thoughts that I have written entire books about it and presented on the subject in many countries. No matter how many words I have now, I still cannot tell you why I am neither a boy nor a girl but also both, even though I have read Judith Butler (and many other gender scholars). The fact is that I just am, and others are too. The best description of my gender is from one of my partners who, upon first meeting me, described me as a "fluffy marshmallow of nonbinary goodness." That and "trans faggot" are two of the best descriptions of my gender, even though I don't usually include them in my bios. I learned early in life that what is accurate, or real, is not always what people want to know.

Gender was/is not the only confounding thing in my life. There are many others, such as the previously mentioned geopolitical borders, the conditional nature of whiteness and oh, so much more. For this essay, though, I am just going to pick on health. Health was also very confusing growing up. I was supposed to eat, but then got picked on for being too fat, even though at that time I wasn't. I loved exercising, but it often brought on pain and injuries. I did what I was supposed to do, but I kept getting sick, mysteriously so, for far too long, no matter how careful I was. It would take nearly three decades for me to be diagnosed with fibromyalgia and hypermobility, and two additional decades for the more encompassing, and accurate, diagnosis of hypermobile Ehlers-Danlos syndrome (hEDS) to be bestowed.

I went from being told that pain was "all in my head" and that I needed to ignore it, and push through, and exercise, to learning that all the yoga I did was not that good for me really. All the running I loved as a teenager and in my 20s had also caused damage in my knees. My stomach started rejecting greens and vegetables. "Healthy" stopped having meaning because no matter how hard I tried, my bodymind would not bend to societal expectations of "healthy actions = healthy consequences." Just like my gender, and my neurotype, my health was mine alone to understand, manage and live with, every day. Just like with gender, with my health I learned more from my fellow humans—that is, people with hEDS, and especially neurodivergent trans people with hEDS and complex PTSD, like myself—than from medical providers. Just like gender, my disabilities were initially invisible to others, although not any longer. Aging with hEDS is not for the faint of heart. Yet, as another partner often says, it's better than the alternative. Sadly, the alternative has found far too many friends already. Both trans and disabled people tend to die before "our time," whatever that expression means, since none of us know how long our time on this good green Earth might be.

I keep finding myself in the liminal spaces, the cracks, the in-between places, but now I know that I am not alone there. These spaces are indeed downright crowded at times! The more I open up about my own experiences, the more I find people who also live in the liminal. Sometimes I wonder if anyone ever feels rested in neat, single boxes or if to be human is to be restless and to long for the liminal space of possibility.

## PART 2

# BEING (TREATED) DIFFERENT

# Do no harm

EDDY SAMARA

I was strapped to the table
waiting for them to run the PIC line
from my elbow to my heart.
The nurse bent over the bracelet that shackled
me to an identity I couldn't
shed despite the fresh scars across my chest.

My smile met hers in a preemptive plea for mercy.
You see, I knew the routine:
She would read the bar-coded band and ask me
to verify my full name—for my protection, of course.

I tried to strike first,
hoping humor would hold the inevitable humiliation in check.
I said, "Yes, that's my Band Name. But please, call me Eddy."
She laughed, but not with me.
"I'm just going to call you by your real name,
Miss So-and-So..."

Tears slid off the table because I couldn't.
I was stuck weighing the relative cost benefit analysis
of pissing off the person pushing a sharp
needle deep into my blood supply,

*All the while speaking blunt trauma into my bones.*

*Now, I would like to tell you*
*that I metaphorically and heroically stood up for myself*
*and for queers everywhere*
*right there in that moment.*
*But that is not my story.*
*That is not the truth.*

*Truth is—I was tired, y'all.*
*I'd been having variations on this demeaning conversation*
*multiple times a day during my hospital stay—*
*courtesy of the finest medical care San Francisco has to offer.*

*Before every blood draw, every test, every procedure,*
*the question of my "real" name?...*
*More times than I can erase*
*someone saying right to my face—*
*essentially—*

*"I refuse to see you."*
*"You do not exist."*
*"You are not a man."*

*In each dismissive refusal to address me properly*
*I heard—repeatedly,*
*I am not even human enough to own my own name.*

*So when the IV tubing stopped just short of my heart,*
*the nurse's words went deeper,*
*tearing into cardiac cavities*
*leaving their echo to beat like an arrhythmia*
*In the hollow space that passes for my chest:*
*I am not a man... I am not a man*
*I am a man... I am a man*
    *I am not a man?*

*I am a man*
  *I am not a man*
*I am a man I am...*
          *I am a man...*
*I am...*

# I am transgender and my disability is not a cautionary tale

FINLAY GAMES

The sharp breeze cuts across the cliff and I tuck my blanket under my thighs a little tighter. I reverse away from the path's edge, back further behind the taller growth of the coarse bushes where it's sheltered. Gently, I lean on the joystick and begin to tentatively bump and roll my way to where my fiancé is throwing a ball for our overly enthusiastic miniature poodle puppy. Life is good.

However, this isn't the life I imagined post gender transition. But then, I didn't take testosterone and have surgery to get a particular kind of life; I did those things to keep my life, to stop life being so painful that all I wanted to do was end it.

Pre-transition, I didn't see a future life at all. Needing to numb the pain I was in, I used anything I could find to escape my body, and to escape the world, even if that escape was only temporary. I found many ways to escape—alcohol, drugs, self-harm, overeating, under-eating, self-neglect, self-abuse. I also tried many times to end my life, coming close many times. Looking back now, it wasn't my life I wanted to end, just the awful pain I was in.

My discovery of myself as transgender came late in life, on the back of getting clean and sober. At the age of 37, knowing finally that I was male, it was only then that I could begin to think about what a future might look like for me. Even then, though, that future wasn't really about material or physical gains; it was about inner emotional and spiritual gains. Boiled down to its simplicity, I wanted an end to the internal torment that I had been trying to run from for my entire life, to no avail. I just wanted to exist in simple peace in myself. I now have that, and so much more, in abundance.

My disability came at the end of my transition, and that was the part of my future that I didn't plan for. I have myalgic encephalomyelitis, otherwise known as chronic fatigue syndrome (ME/CFS), which is a neurological energy-limiting condition affecting every bodily system. There are still many unknowns in the causes of ME/CFS, but it's thought to be caused by a virus, an infection, trauma, genetics, or a combination of these.

I was diagnosed with ME/CFS in 2022, though I had been experiencing symptoms since 2017. My GP first diagnosed me with hypothyroidism, but even when that was managed with medication, my extreme fatigue remained. Finally, a new GP recognized that all my other classic symptoms pointed towards ME/CFS. I also have postural orthostatic tachycardia syndrome (PoTS), which causes me to have issues with a high heart rate (tachycardia), dizziness, poor temperature control, and migraines, among many other things! All these combined leave me needing to lead a very slow-paced life. I'm now restricted with my mobility, and I use an electric wheelchair outside the house to help with the immediate fatigue and dizziness, and to conserve my limited energy.

The hardest part of being both transgender and disabled is that I am constantly judged, mostly by individuals in the gender-critical camp, on my success as a transitioned person, based solely on my physical capabilities and health. Even worse than this, my disability is often used by them as a weapon, as "proof" as to why gender transition is harmful.

It is impossible to say that my gender transition, taking hormones and having surgeries, caused my chronic illness. That people want to make such an implausible and incorrect direct correlation is short-sighted and overly simplistic.

I should add that those trying to draw this non-existent straight line from gender transition to my being chronically ill and disabled are rarely those who are medically qualified. Rather, it is those who are heavily invested in invalidating trans identities and the joy and freedom that gender transition gives so many of us.

Even well-meaning people, on learning that I am disabled with a chronic illness, will often ask if I regret my transition, or if I have considered stopping taking my hormone replacement therapy (testosterone). It hurts deeply that the first thing they blame in my life is my transition and the first thing they consider as the solution is to put a stop to it. The problem is that the narrative of gender transition as dangerous, medically unsound, and nothing more than body mutilation is so pervasive in the media. It's all too easy to just hear this side of the story and believe it, so I am more forgiving of well-meaning friends, who just want to help, but I educate them, nonetheless.

I have, of course, tried to work out what might have caused me to develop ME/CFS, but it really is impossible to answer. I have an incredibly complex health history. Growing up in the 1980s as I did, with low information and high stigma around LGBTQ identities, I didn't know that I was transgender. Therefore, with my gender dysphoria undiagnosed, that early distress turned into full-blown severe mental health issues. Unable to cope with the pain I was in, then followed drug and alcohol misuse, self-harm, and eating disorders. All these caused huge trauma to my body and would have severely weakened my immune and nervous system, making me a prime target for chronic illness. Then, although a positive move, going through recovery, getting sober and clean and rebuilding my life, was another huge mental and physical stress. On top of this, it's also just as likely to be my genetics. My mum had hypothyroidism and Addison's disease, and I've already inherited hypothyroidism from her. So, while it is possible that surgery during gender transition and infections during my lower surgery may then have triggered the ME/CFS, there are so many other factors. No straight line exists here at all!

But is working out what caused my chronic illness really important now? Why play the blame game? It's only to serve a purpose of blaming my transition and to use my disability as a cautionary tale—"Look, he transitioned and now he's in a wheelchair!"—as if it was a direct link, and as if using a wheelchair makes me a lesser human being.

The same thing is often said about the way I look. "Gender transition has really aged you." No, my friend, *time* has aged me: I was 37 when I began my transition. I am 49 now. Before hormone therapy, trans men in particular look incredibly young. Once on testosterone, we catch up, Now I just look my age. Because of transition, I now get to age, I'm going to get even older, I'll get age-related illness, and my body will become frail. That's not due to gender transition; that's life, that's aging. I'm blessed now to take part in that process.

If we are going to play the blame game, I would like to point out two particularly important points that are often not considered. The first is that it is true that trans people do have a higher incidence of chronic illness and disability. However, this is not an inherent part of, or caused by, being trans, but rather a product of the world we live in.

Using my own life as an example, had there been more

awareness of trans people when I was growing up, had there been more support, I might not have developed such severe mental health problems. Had I been able to transition earlier, had there been prompt access to healthcare, I might not have needed to escape the pain of gender dysphoria by turning to alcohol, drugs, self-harm, and disordered eating. If the medical profession had more knowledge and understanding of transgender healthcare, I would have had more support and better aftercare post-surgery and might not have developed infections. If we lived in a world where being trans wasn't such a sentence of stigma and discrimination, then all this stress and trauma might have been avoided, and so might the ME/CFS. This is true for all trans people who suffer the stress of living in a world with a lack of support and high incidences of stigma and discrimination. The negative impact on the health and wellbeing in our community due to this is profound.

And the second is that if I was anyone other than a trans person, this conversation of blame wouldn't be happening. Let's not forget that gender transition is lifesaving treatment for the vast majority of transgender people. It certainly was for me. As with many lifesaving treatments, it comes with some risks, and when the benefits outweigh those risks, we take them willingly. I'm alive today because of transition. Had I not transitioned, I wouldn't have ME/CFS because I would not be alive.

Countless people have treatment and surgeries every day, but they are supported because people recognize the need. The fundamental difference is that most of the population do not recognize gender transition as lifesaving treatment or may even view it as a fad or, worse, body mutilation. Therefore, instead of being supported through any complications or difficulties, even ones that are not linked, we are blamed for transitioning. We are blamed for having lifesaving treatment.

Even if my gender transition did cause my ME/CFS, I

wouldn't change a thing, because my life now, even with ME/CFS, is a million times better than it was before transition. And besides, having ME/CFS, being disabled, and using a wheelchair do not negate the fact that I am a happily transitioned man.

Of course, it isn't easy living with chronic illness. The pain, fatigue, and myriad of other symptoms that show up daily are tough to handle. However, what makes it harder is the combination of being transgender and disabled. For all the reasons I've already mentioned, there is the instant judgment that as a disabled trans person I must have somehow brought this on myself, but also the double stigma.

Dealing with the stigma around disability—especially an invisible condition like ME/CFS which still gets misrepresented—adds another layer of trauma into the mix. The constant medical gaslighting, the lack of public awareness, the lack of access to treatment, it's a merry-go-round of discrimination and stigma.

This "stigma stacking," as I like to call it, is a heavy burden to carry, oftentimes heavier than the actual symptoms of my chronic illness. The constant devaluing of both of my main identities. The relentless microaggressions of transphobia and ableism. These perpetuate the trauma and the stress, and keep my nervous system in fight and flight, which does my chronic illness no good whatsoever.

So yes, being transgender and disabled is incredibly hard, but it isn't these identities themselves that make life hard as much as the way the world views and treats me for having them. If you were to take this out of the trans and disabled cauldron, we would all be a happier, healthier community for sure.

However, the positive side is that being transgender and being disabled are two interlinked identities of which I am incredibly proud. Because of being transgender, I have had no choice but to learn to be strong, resilient, and compassionate. Because of my disability I have had to learn to be resourceful, adaptive, and patient. These identities have pushed me to be a better person and connected me to a community of the most loving, generous, and loyal people. These identities have also connected me to a unique way of being in this world, one where identity is expansive, and your value isn't tied to your output.

What matters now is how I live with ME/CFS. Completing my gender transition is one of the strongest factors in living well with ME/CFS. This is because my mental health is better, as is my desire to live, to look after myself, to have hope, purpose, and desire for the future. All these exist because I have transitioned, and these are strong pillars of wellness that get me through every single day.

I didn't want a perfect life; I just wanted a life and couldn't have one before because the pain got in the way, the desire to end it got in the way. I got what I wanted, a life, and now it's about taking that life I've been given on its terms. My life is full. I have a fiancé I love, friends who are like family, and when I laugh, it's with complete abandon. I am clean and sober. I can get out in nature—it's on four wheels, but so what?! I need more rest than most folks, and I must go a lot slower, but that's not necessarily a terrible thing. Our society is so invested in being on the go, viewing resting as bad, and I've now escaped that. I get to live at my own pace and just sit and watch the world I'm blessed to live in.

Being disabled is just another thing I've come to love about myself, like my being transgender. I didn't want to be transgender, but it's who I am. Gradually, I found the courage to accept it, to transition, and then I discovered a world of happiness on the other side. Likewise, I didn't expect to be disabled, but I've accepted it and, with adjustments, I've discovered ways to be happy and free and equally proud.

# Swimming westward away

LAWRENCE LORRAINE MULLEN

*from disjointed / disproportionate*
*anatomical orange*
*asking others if they too*
*have removed their bruises*
*their internal stitches*
*with a pair of scissors and a scalpel*
*or let them dissolve*
*sinking back into the bloodstream*

*sepsis isn't static*
*and neither are your arms*
*forward the sun is rising in silence*
*and setting in copper.*

# Bathroom buzz cut

LIZ MOORE

The first time I shaved my head, my doctor assumed I had been in an auto accident. Or maybe had brain surgery.

Something medical that necessitated cutting into my skull, and therefore required the pre-op nurse to remove my hair before coating my skull in betadine.

My doctor laughed awkwardly when I explained I just wanted to shave my head, while my theyfriend helped me walk to the exam room.

* * *

It is very hard to get a queer haircut from a suburban hair salon. Or barber shop. It doesn't really matter. Everyone thinks you don't know what you want, and they insist on making it more feminine. Longer, with a blow dryer to add more body.

Yet another attempt. Yet another poofy pixie cut full of hairspray. Trying not to cry in front of anyone, though my face goes red and blotchy. The car. My theyfriend. Sobbing, again.

And so I find myself having that quintessentially queer experience of sitting naked in the bathroom while my lover shaves my head.

* * *

Growing up, I had long, flowing hair. Girls in school would ask to play with my hair, and I would relish the fluttery feeling I got when they ran their fingers through my hair as they braided it.

The girl I dated at summer camp thought I was straight because of my long hair, even though I had it pulled back with a rainbow headband. "When I first saw you, I thought, 'She has no idea what that rainbow means,'" she told me as we lay entwined in bed.

* * *

Middle school afternoons. The library, reading through back issues of *Seventeen* and *Cosmo* like I was cramming for a final exam.

A kid in school called me a fag for the way I dressed. A kid at camp called me a dyke because I didn't shave my legs.

If I can just mold myself into someone they will accept, maybe it will stop.

Nothing to see here. Just a teenage girl doing normal teenage girl things.

I manage to be just normal enough to fit in with the theater kids, my hair tied back in a messy bun.

* * *

Yesterday's theater kids all cluster together in the campus Pride group.

I think this is belonging.

A group of us are talking about gender, like you do. My

stomach is fluttering as I confess I am maybe trans. It is the first time I have said it out loud.

The trans guy I have a crush on glances skeptically at my hair, before going back to talking about HRT. His look says, "You have no idea what that means."

And I don't think he knows what I mean. I was not born in the wrong body. I don't want to take HRT. But I'm not this package of assumptions people make when they look at my hair. M? No. F? No. None of the above. All of the above?

\* \* \*

Each time my theyfriend shaves off my hair, I feel lighter. Not just the physical weight of my hair. But like this time, I am shucking off the too-tight mask spun from teen magazines.

Yet when I step outside, the weight of gender expectations still tugs on the short stubble of my hair. "Excuse me, sir." Polo shirts and cargo pants. "Young man." A startled glance between my skirt and my hair. A crawling sort of wrongness.

The clerk who stammers, "Have a nice day, sir. Er, ma'am?"

And I think: yes. A fluttering laugh pulls at my throat. Sir, er, ma'am? That's me.

\* \* \*

I'm sitting in a barber shop in Provincetown, just down the road from a monument to colonizing Pilgrims and several drag bars.

Everyone in the room is gay. My barber runs his hands through my hair and sighs when I tell him I just want something easy. "But your hair is so beautiful! Are you sure you don't want to use just a little bit of gel?"

Here it comes, I thought. I'm going to be overruled on my hair yet again.

"I don't want to fuss with a blow dryer or mousse or anything. Just shower and dry my hair. Just something easy and gay," I say, and everyone laughs.

"Oh, easy and gay, hmm?"

"Sounds perfect," I say. And it is.

I think this is what they mean by gender euphoria, this feeling of sea breezes flowing through my hair. The nod of recognition I give when I see another queer person, and they see me. The visceral pleasure when my lover tugs my hair in the dark, and a moan reverberates through us both.

In a few short weeks, my hair has grown out once again. Except I am back in the suburbs, and very far from my trio of P-town barbers.

\* \* \*

This is how I style my hair: sitting on the toilet seat, my they-friend running the razor over the tufts behind my ears. Just a buzz cut that slowly grows out into something nameless and spiky.

A shaggy mullet or maybe a bob, depending on how long we wait till my next buzz cut. When you shave your hair at home, you have to clean up the floor yourself. In this house, no one has the energy to clean hair clippings off the bathroom floor.

We let our hair morph and grow, until suddenly it's too much: too much work, too long, too femme, too itchy, too something. Enough to make it worth moving the cats' litterbox out of the bathroom so it doesn't get filled with little splinters of hair.

Lather, rinse, repeat. Long and short and back again. Lather, rinse, repeat.

Femme and masc and somewhere in between. Hair-flux. Buzz-fluid. It feels comfortable here. And if it starts to feel too constraining, I can just shave it all off again.

* * *

I dyed my hair blue for the first and last time. The color bleeds on my towel, but that's not why I'm planning to stop.

I finally have a diagnosis after years of pain and "maybe it's autoimmune" and "oh, your tests are normal." OK, sure, C-reactive protein and white blood count and sed rate are all elevated. But those are non-specific markers of inflammation. Who knows why it's elevated, probably just stress. That white blood count is just normal for you.

Except, apparently, it is my immune system—just not quite an autoimmune disorder. My doctor calls it immune dysregulation, or Mast Cell Activation Syndrome. Whatever. My immune system wants to challenge everything to a duel.

And I do mean everything: fragrances, coffee, toilet paper, my anti-inflammatory pain cream.

A friend of mine has the same condition and always dyed their hair with the same brand of dye. It was fine until it wasn't and they ended up hospitalized for an anaphylactic reaction to their (permanent) hair dye.

I take plenty of pictures with my blue hair. I give myself a jagged undercut (and shoulder pain) and take more. "I could have helped," my theyfriend says. But I want this one, this one haircut, to be all mine.

I try to tattoo the memory into my mind. The feeling of this gender, this hair, this dye. Of the razor in my hand, buzzing against my skull.

The thing about gender euphoria is that it doesn't last. Euphoria is a transient emotion. Memories don't always last, either, but I try to hold on to this one.

* * *

No matter what I do, my hair hurts. There is pain pulsing in each follicle. My immune system would like to register a complaint about the ingredients in every hair product in existence. I use the least painful one, but I'm still left with a rash after every shower.

Showering. Hold the grab bar and try not to fall. The door left open in case I need to call for help. Sagging on the shower chair as the water washes away my energy. Sometimes I have a "rinse" instead of a shower, just letting the water wash over me. If I lift my arms to wash my hair, I might not be able to dry myself off. My theyfriend helping me lift my leg over the tub and drying me off with a towel.

My hair clearly has to go.

The friction of the razor raises little hives across my scalp. This time it is surgical. Not so that a surgeon can cut into my brain. I am excising one item from my to-do list. I am shaving off the part of me that had energy for hair care.

Lather, rinse, repeat. No more mullets or even shaggy pixies. I exist somewhere between bald and a shaggy halo of hair, in the stretch of hallway between my bed and the bathroom.

* * *

My immune system is apparently dueling every other cell in my body. I thought I knew what fatigue was, but this?

Spending the day in bed because I thought too much. I tried to refill my meds and then something stuttered in my brain, shut down, a pain. Error 404, blue screen of death. Not dead, but suspended in a perpetual load screen.

And all I can do is curl up in the dark and the quiet and wait for it to pass. Can't talk without slurring, without slurring, without without...

Don't even have words for texting, for those apps, those

speech-to-text apps. Just me in the dark, and I can't even get upset about it because crying takes energy I don't have.

My theyfriend would hold me but I can't bear to be touched.

But some days, there is room for dreaming. I rifle through my memories, like a dusty old card catalog full of who I used to be. Blue hair and an undercut. Sea breezes and gender euphoria. My theyfriend's hands in my hair.

* * *

When you are housebound, so much of your social interactions are clinical. A blood draw, an MRI, the emergency room. Another specialist, another referral. Lather, rinse, repeat.

I have long flowing hair and have managed to bathe. They see a white woman, with all the privileges and assumptions that entails. My blood tests are normal. There is mild degeneration on my MRI, but that's normal for my age. I am anxious or attention seeking. I need to exercise more. It's just deconditioning. No pain, no gain. I am preoccupied with health concerns. A prescription for physical therapy. Diet and exercise. Hysteria.

My head is shaved, and I'm wearing the kind of shapeless sack marketed as "androgynous" because it's the least painful article of clothing I own. I am white, but not the right kind of woman. I would not blend in at a country club. I drag my lower body into the office with my walker. So how long have you been on narcotics? I am not on narcotics. Have you ever been on narcotics? Why do you take so many medications? Who prescribes all these? Who sent you? Why are you traveling so far for medical care? How many doctors have you seen? What do you expect me to do for you? Why are you here? Malingering.

* * *

My brain. There are hours when the fog is just a mist. I make conversation with the nurse who gives me my monthly biologic injections, and I cobble the words together in order mostly.

The injections are helping. The insurance that covers the $2000-a-month injections is helping. Having family to drive me several hours to the monthly $2000 injections is helping.

I have tried so many things, and some of them are helping. Supplements and teas and medical diets. Pacing, always pacing to try to avoid the crash. Fragrance-free shampoo that my immune system doesn't try to challenge to a duel.

So many things are still bad, but they are less bad. There are more hours before my brain freezes like an old laptop. I still can't do basic arithmetic, but I can hug my theyfriend. Some days, I can write.

My scalp doesn't feel as though it's been flayed by a razor's edge. I am afraid to hope.

I let my hair grow like it is a delicate orchid. Temperamental, fragile, precious. Ephemeral. I do not know how long I will be able to bear the weight of it. I do not know if I will be able to grow my hair ever again.

I sense a fluttering sort of joy in running my hands through my hair. I have a streak of white near my witch's peak, like Morticia Addams. Like a scar flowing through my hair, saying: I survived. I survive.

# What I remember

MAXWELL COLLETTI VON RAVEN

## Part 1

I remember my flip-flops on the sidewalk as I waited for my dog to have his morning go. Still half asleep and lost in the sound of his snuffling and the smell of fresh-baked bread on a dry autumn breeze.

I remember thinking, "Wow, I feel weird," and my mind drifted, and I was standing on the porch of my house in New Mexico in the mountains, waiting for Ogi, my dog, to come back in, and then I heard the sound of a car drive by, and I wasn't sure where I was now. Mountain cabin in New Mexico? Outside my apartment in Minneapolis? Oh shit, I didn't know! Panicking, I opened my eyes wide for some confirmation and orientation, and uh, yeah, still darkness, still blind—well, crap. Ogi trotted up to me in his elderly way, and I said, "Inside, buddy. Let's go," and I followed him inside to what turned out to be my apartment in Minneapolis. I had had some weird days in the six months since brain surgery, but this was extreme weirdness.

What I remember is a few hours later, sitting in the cramped waiting area outside the clinic's lab, fidgeting with my folded-up white cane. Turns out, even though the flashy brain tumor and its abnormal cells get all the attention at first, the complications I don't remember anyone mentioning steal the show when you survive. As in, after brain surgery, my pituitary gland stopped functioning. So, my partner and I were waiting on the results of stat bloodwork, trying to figure out what was going on with my precarious science experiment of a body. The doctor came out. From her tone as she greeted us, we knew she did not have good news.

Max, your sodium is 118. You need to go to the ER.

Oh, crap, really? Dammit. Do I have to?

Yes.

Can I go home first and grab a phone charger and some comfortable shorts and...

No, you need to go directly to the ER. In fact, I'm not really sure how you're even standing and walking around and talking right now.

Emergency room. The dangers of low sodium. Transness. Uncomfortable problems, awkward explanations, and reasonable fears. An ER is a place a trans person goes reluctantly.

I can't forget the range of medical encounters as a queer and trans young adult. Being refused treatment, being ignored, being regarded as less than human, being called disgusting, and, more than 20 years later, still being dismissed and misdiagnosed.

The first signs of the brain tumor were imaged on CT and MRI. It was seven years before I got the correct diagnosis. It's just a mucilaginous cyst; don't worry about it, they said. No, we don't know why you have nearly constant migraines or why your field of vision is shrinking. Must be that testosterone you take because you're trans.

As the years went by, I continued to accumulate new weird symptoms, and various medical professionals continue to blow me off, treat me as if I were drug-seeking and scrounging for pain meds, or simply dismiss me, as though all of my symptoms were due to psychological problems. I remember that sometime around the holidays in 2016, I finally ended up with a good primary care doctor who sent me to a neurologist for an MRI to rule out MS.

I remember sitting next to my partner in the neurologist office, explaining all of my symptoms to him, how everything had developed over time, my partner chiming in to help me remember some of the details that I wasn't tracking. After we finished explaining, the doctor took over.

And who is this next to you?

This is my partner, Eddy.

Do you have AIDS?

No.

Well, I think you need to get an AIDS test. And you probably just need to get B12 shots. I bet you have low B12.

I was stunned and unsure how to respond, but Eddy, in his signature direct communication style, reminded him I was there for an MS rule-out, and based on the symptoms, the protocol is ordering an MRI. After more pushing and advocating, the doctor agreed to order the MRI but repeated he thought I just needed to go get an AIDS test. I still can't fathom why a doctor in the year 2016 still used the phrase "AIDS test." After the MRI, the doctor called me to inform me about the mass that was found on imaging, what he thought it was, and that it still didn't explain my headaches, and yes, I should still get a B12 shot. He referred me to neurosurgery with a non-urgent diagnosis. My next follow-up appointment with neurosurgery would be three or four months away.

Luckily, I got a second opinion.

## Part 2

I was born with a rare retinal condition, called FEVR, which, by now, left me with no usable vision, just a small amount of light perception in one eye. Fortunately, I guess, the tumor was smashing my optic nerve, so when I brought the scan results to my retina specialist, he referred me to a colleague in neurosurgery who specializes in tumors in the skull base.

In the next two weeks, they ordered a more detailed MRI on a fancier machine, I was assigned a care team, I met with the neurosurgeon who correctly diagnosed my tumor, and I was scheduled for brain surgery.

I had a craniopharyngioma. The subtype is normally found in children and adolescents. I was in my mid-30s but, apparently, late onset happens sometimes. The tumor was on my pituitary stalk, smashing my pituitary backwards, smashing the optic nerve, and pushing on the hypothalamus, which is just above the pituitary stalk. It needed to come out soon before it caused any more collateral damage, and before it grew too large to remove through the nose.

My memories of this period are very foggy, like a long, weird dream you can't wake up from. Literally. It was hard to stay awake during the day. I had a constant migraine. I remember being worried that my trans status might be a problem every time I had to meet a new doctor. Yet I also remember being pleasantly surprised that my being trans was not a problem at all with my new care team. Not that it should have been a problem, of course, though it often is.

I remember it was early March when they sent the robots in through my right nostril. They drilled a hole through my skull in the back of my sinuses and then used lasers to remove all the tumor cells they could find from my pituitary stalk and brain. They hauled the abnormal cells back out through my nose and patched up both the hole in my brain and the hole that went through my skull. I had some complications and ended up staying in the hospital for a little over three weeks, but I can remember just a handful of negative interactions with nursing staff based on my being trans. These were typically related to a new nurse coming on shift and using the wrong pronouns for me; they would either correct themselves or they would disappear soon.

For a good portion of this hospital stay, I thought my room was a beachside resort with palm trees over my bed, the sounds of seagulls and crashing waves, and the scent of fresh, tropical breeze. Or I was in a rainforest.

It's possible, though a generous interpretation, that my memory is faulty. More likely, my bar for medical professionals is low. Eddy would remember this time very differently. In fact, I suspect he is the reason the offensive nurses disappeared.

Every hospital, every ER, every clinic, every doctor, every nurse is like a gamble, more so for some identities than others and more so for those of us in the intersections. Who will treat me like a human being and who will not? What would an odds maker say?

There is the narrative that as time moves forward, civil and human rights will become a universal priority. But this is naïve. It's still a gamble for every trans person who needs to access healthcare. In fact, though awareness and respect have grown, the odds always favor the house.

I don't actually remember how I got to the ER that morning when my sodium was 118. I don't remember how long we had to wait before going back to the little cubicle room. I do remember the ER staff lost the first round of bloodwork because they forgot to label the vials of blood before sending them through the magical medical pneumatic tubes. And I remember Eddy by my side the whole time. And I remember my primary care doctor coming by to see me and hearing her advocate for me with the ER staff. I remember feeling frustrated and confused. I remember trying to explain to multiple people that I was a brain tumor survivor and had just had brain surgery six months earlier, and as a result, I have a lot of complex endocrine-related conditions now, so they needed to consult someone from endocrinology before coming up with a treatment plan or they would easily kill me.

I know Eddy had contacted my regular endocrinologist to let her know I was going to the ER with low sodium. She gave us her cell phone number to have the attending doctor contact her to talk about my complicated case. I think that the longer I sat on the uncomfortable hospital gurney, entangled in wires attached to beeping machines, the more it dawned on me that I indeed felt pretty weird and not OK.

One of the side effects of low sodium is hallucinations. For me, they were brightly colored, ever-changing images swirling in the darkness. That is my lack of sight with an accompaniment of weird ethereal music playing in the back of my head. Since this had happened before, when I was in the hospital after my brain surgery, I wasn't surprised by it, but it is still very distracting. I was in a jungle or maybe a rainforest. There were plants, trees, brightly colored birds dancing amid the undulating, multicolored ferns and fronds.

I remember a knock and the sound of the sliding door of my cubicle opening, pulling my attention out of the rainforest dance party. I heard a new, confident-sounding doctor voice. It was the voice of the head of the endocrinology department.

He introduced himself and the small pack of med students who were following him around for the day. I'm not sure how many there were—at least three or four people; it sounded like a crowd of tourists had scrunched itself into my little stall.

I started reciting my explanation of how I had ended up here today, how low my sodium had been at the clinic earlier, and the symptoms I was experiencing. I explained that I have panhypopituitarism since the brain surgery. In concert with that, I was concerned with adrenal insufficiency and diabetes insipidus, which was likely the root of the low sodium. I remember feeling that I was explaining things well, despite all of the dancing plants and animals.

I heard the clicking and typing sounds of him pulling up my chart on the computer.

So what's your surgery status?

Well, they took the tumor out.

No, no, I mean your trans surgery status?

(Me, confused) I don't really think that's relevant, but it should all be in my chart. I had top surgery like 15 years ago and I have not had a hysterectomy.

I don't clearly remember what happened after this, other than my absolute bafflement. I remember thinking that it was lucky that I am comfortable talking about my trans status in the context of medical history. Had I not been, it could have been much more awkward, even destabilizing. I ended up staying in the hospital for ten days, having to interact with this doctor, always with the lingering feelings of awkward vulnerability. Now I know that I should not have answered his question. That I should have stopped talking after saying, "I don't really think that's relevant."

I remember this hospital stay as a constant struggle, even with the presence of some excellent nurses. I remember several big mistakes made because some of the doctors would not listen to me or Eddy. When we explained my condition, they didn't take us seriously or they were too overconfident and arrogant to admit they didn't actually know what to do and were resistant to having my regular endocrinologist consult on my case. I remember the relief at finally being discharged: they hadn't caused permanent brain damage or killed me.

I remember, too, lying half awake/half asleep in the hospital bed, listening to TV news coverage of Hurricane Harvey pummeling the Texas coast, where I grew up. I was thinking, wow, I know how that feels. The inevitability of the storm making landfall and the precariousness of being a little human in the force of a massive looming storm. Will the flood waters wash me away completely? Will I get a good power-washing and come away unscathed? There's no way to know beforehand.

## Part 3

I have trans broken arm syndrome. Most trans folks have it, even if they don't know they do. With trans broken arm syndrome, your medical provider is so preoccupied with your transness that they fail to treat or they misdiagnose the obvious presenting problem. The root cause of every medical problem is your trans status, hormone therapy, or trans-related surgeries. For example, doctors explain that the reason my sodium level was 118 is because I am trans. I was first diagnosed with trans broken arm syndrome when I came out as a young adult, so I was not really surprised the doctor felt he needed to know the configuration of the plumbing of my body before he could address the problem of why my sodium was 118.

On the other hand, on the handful of occasions that my trans status hasn't come up—such as when I am alone, without my partner, and the providers assume I am a cisgender, straight dude—I get treated very differently. It's still a game of chance, with the variables being how you are perceived and which provider happens to be working with you.

I wish I had something more hopeful to say, after nearly a quarter century of being queer/trans and trying to access what should be a human right—basic health care. I think it's scarier than it was back then, back when we were invisible, simply didn't exist, and people didn't understand what the hell I was. Now, we trans folks are political, conservative, religious targets. We receive clear and direct hatred and malice, unambiguous threats of violence, and we are the focus of laws designed to deny us access to healthcare, to respect, to visibility, to basic human rights.

In my more cynical moments, I think, "This is how they're going to get rid of us all! They're going to block our access to antibiotics, vaccines, and preventative cancer screenings." Isn't legally denying access to gender-affirming care via purposeful cruelty terrible enough? I never would have thought that ringing the little bell at successfully completing radiation treatment would be a radical act. I never thought not dying would be the radical act it has been.

# New disease

NOVA LARKIN SCHRAGE

*You always said that*
*people have sexes"*
*what it means*
*to assign me to a gender*
*to label my emotions*
*disordered, to allot me*
*per year, to ask that my name*
*correct*

*"words have genders,*
*and I've been thinking about*
*to be a prescriptivist:*
*"for insurance purposes,"*
*subclinical, my behavior*
*40 hours of sick time*
*auto-*
*to yours.*

*//*

*A lover once told me that*
*grow into easy adults,*
*into difficult adults"*
*what it means*
*how sometimes the form*
*(mobility, auditory,*
*visual) and I*
*all my cookies.*
*and let one*
*from my fingers*
*as I walk home*
*to go mad*

*"difficult children*
*while easy children grow*
*and I've been thinking about*
*to be non-binary:*
*only has two options*
*thinking/learning,*
*quit. I erase*
*I tear up the form*
*small strip slip*
*every few blocks*
*alone. I've tried*
*as quietly as possible.*

I've tried  
to deserve accommodations  
the paperwork. I  
I'm on medical leave, because  
while asking about my vacation  

to be disabled enough  
but abled enough to complete  
haven't told you  
isn't misgendering me  
what's easiest for you?  

//

You always said that  
people *get angry*"  
what  
means  
                to be  

"cows go mad,  
and I've been thinking about  
it  

a dead cow  
a crazy bitch—  

to have to teach myself  
"help"  
reading  

how to spell  
without a doctor  
"hospitalize."

# COVID-19, self-revelations, and the resilience of intersectional online community

JAC (THEY/THEM) OF GENDERMEOWSTER

My world got bigger in March of 2020 when the worldwide COVID-19 lockdowns began. So many people felt trapped and isolated, but I suddenly had an infusion of friends, and a whole new purpose in life. Let me explain! First, you need a bit of my own story, then I'll connect it to bigger concepts.

I am a white, disabled, non-binary, AuDHD step-parent, in my mid-30s, living in the Northwestern United States. I was working from home long before the lockdowns started. I didn't realize it at the time, but I needed mobility aids. Since I didn't have them, most of my socializing was online. So when suddenly people who had never used Zoom or Discord or watched a stream on Twitch were online—because they were home, bored, and lonely—the friends I'd once had when

I was able to work out of the house and go out dancing were suddenly accessible again.

There was a renaissance of wonderful and weird art being made by folks who could not work. Our pets and children became our co-workers while the whole world learned how to work from home. We[1] played TTRPGs. We started podcasts. We got pregnant. We wrote poetry books, started huge crafting projects, and learned to bake bread. Support groups moved online, and recovery became that much more accessible to the masses. The government gave everyone money in the form of "COVID relief payments." We suddenly had a small form of Universal Basic Income, and everyone got to work from home, tend their children, and have more flexibility with labor than many had experienced before.

The lockdowns were also a time of deep self-reflection, especially for folks who were in lockdown by themselves or solely with a partner. I know I had multiple awakenings that started around that time and rolled out over the next couple of years.

I had been identifying as non-binary since early 2017 and had already changed my name and transitioned as non-binary socially, but during the first year of lockdowns, I slowly began to unmask: layers of behavior built to appease neurotypicals—from mirroring a smile back at people at the right, expected moments to suppressing the desire to listen to or watch things while I worked—slowly fell away. The only other person in the house[2] was the trans woman who would become my wife. For the first time, I could just exist. And I had many soul-crushing,

---

1    Essential workers missed out on most or all of this and risked their lives to keep many of us fed and medicated. Thank you, essential workers. I grieve all of you who died before the vaccine was available. This subject is perhaps also beyond the scope of this essay.

2    Most of the time, I have step-children who visit every other weekend. Hi, kids!

terror-filled evenings that I *might* be autistic.[3] My wife was very supportive. She told me that if I *was* autistic, me realizing it just gave a name to something that was already true. I slowly made peace with this realization.

We were married October 10th, 2020, on the last sunny day of the year. The rain started two hours after the ceremony while we were driving home, and it didn't stop for several months. We married for many reasons—love, health insurance, and fear of being separated by governmental authorities if we had to flee transmisic[4] violence in the United States, being just a few. Our fear was not unfounded. Three months later, on January 6th, 2021, while my wife was being wheeled in to have her bottom surgery,[5] armed people organized and executed an insurrection—storming the national and multiple state capitols in the United States. It was a terrifying time for many of us, made worse for those who were trans[6] and disabled (in that moment, post-op, my wife was also temporarily disabled while recovering from surgery). I remember staying in our accommodations and avoiding any outside contact whenever possible. It just didn't feel safe to be visibly trans in the Republican town we were in for her procedure.

The next whammy would come two months later. Even

---

3    For legal reasons relating to ableist laws that prevent some basic human rights for people with autism, it feels important to me to mention that I've never received a formal diagnosis of autism. I self-identify that way, based on what I've seen in the broader autistic community. This self-identification helps me find ways to cope with my neurotype without making myself vulnerable to the negative legal repercussions of a formal diagnosis.

4    Transmisia is the hatred of trans people. It is an alternate to the word "transphobia" because the suffix -phobia means fear and -misia means hatred. This is a contested term. https://translanguageprimer.com/transmisia

5    The vlog about her bottom surgery experiences is here: www.youtube.com/playlist?list=PLRxYpHg9FcZB3x7TRoCH918aNPBLThRFn

6    I tend to use "trans" expansively as a short hand for transgender, nonbinary, agender, two-spirit, and other gender-diverse identities.

though I had socially transitioned, I had come to a point where I realized I wanted to start hormone replacement therapy (HRT). Cue crippling anxiety round two! My wife—a self-described "transbian"—was not into masculine-presenting folks. I was terrified! Did I have to choose between medicine that might make my dysphoria go away, that might make my brain work better and me feel more confident in myself, and this wonderful woman who loved me and was the most supportive and kind person I had ever dated?

Thankfully, it turned out, I did not. Trans for Trans (T4T) relationships are magical. She understood (and still understands) the critical and deep importance of having access to HRT if your brain has dysphoria and needs it. She just wanted me to be happy.

I had my first dose of testosterone on March 11th, 2021—a year to the day after the World Health Organization declared COVID-19 an official pandemic.

The following years included more trans surgeries[7]—both hers and mine. We bought our first house with all the funds we could muster. We adopted two more cats[8] that became fast friends. My wife realized she was somewhere in the ace-spec/demi-sexual spectrum, while I slowly realized that T was making me more gay-man-flavored sexually while still being panromantic. That was perhaps the scariest realization of all! She very lovingly accepts this about me, and we have since opened our relationship to polyamory and I have some lovely partners who also happen to be non-binary.

---

7   We kept vlogs of our first surgeries, but we were not as vigilant with record keeping for later procedures. You can see my top surgery records here: www.youtube.com/playlist?list=PLRxYpHg9FcZB2y_5i67ura bbl_XAq6Tyi

8   Neferkitty (she/her, calico) is my oldest cat, she is 11 years old as of this writing. The "kittens" (now just over a year old) are Beatrix (she/per, orange tabby) and Cleocatra (she/fae, calico).

This long, winding story serves a deeper purpose (besides demonstrating my ADHD). During *all* of the experiences I described above, I had a community supporting me: from realizing my neurotype, to getting married, to starting HRT, to buying a home, to reconsidering my sexual and romantic orientation. I had an online community of disabled, queer, trans and gender-diverse, and neurodivergent (or neurospicy as we like to say) folks. Many of these realizations I described above were later recorded in my "non-binary HRT check-ins"[9]—a weekly, then monthly, vlog I recorded during the opening sequence of the newly minted Genderful podcast. There is even footage of my wedding on YouTube—you can go watch it![10] We recorded it not only for ourselves, but also as an example of a trans, pagan wedding. Getting married during a pandemic felt like a cultural moment worth preserving! Multiple friends have benefited from imagining a break from tradition that might be something approximately like this.

Making content during the lockdowns, and continuing to do so now, has served to connect me with so many wonderful people across the world that I may not have otherwise known. It started as a Twitch stream, and evolved into a Discord community (Meowster's Clowder, or just The Clowder) podcast, hub for solidarity resources, and vehicle for fundraising for disabled and trans people through Mutual Aid.[11]

Here's a few of the things I've learned over the past few years: **Disabled community thrives online.** The internet gives

9  A playlist of my video diary entries can be found here: www.youtube.com/playlist?list=PLRxYpHg9FcZCECBFdIgyuxCaCe2giJLPY
10 This is not my most polished content, but it is some of the most special content we have ever made: www.youtube.com/watch?v=THFBvn47N2U&t=5s
11 Alex Iantaffi (the editor of this anthology) and I spoke at length about this community on their podcast, Gender Stories. You can listen to it on all major podcasting platforms. Here is the episode with the transcript: https://genderstories.buzzsprout.com/156032/13264531-building-a-web-of-care-with-gendermeowster

isolated, disabled people a way to socialize from the comfort of their homes. We can be having a low-spoons day and still have accessible ways to participate in community. We can even work together for the greater good by organizing mutual aid events for one another online. To date, the most successful event I've co-organized was Kaemsi Mutual Aid. We planned it for about six months and raised $17,042.10 over a three-day live-stream raid train event, plus donations before and after the event. In fact, we raised so much money that we not only fully funded Kaemsi's solar panels,[12] but we also raised enough money for me to buy my first (and currently only) wheelchair. It was totally incredible and surprising and rewarding to bring that many wonderful people together for a good cause.

**Trans community thrives online.** Gender-diverse and trans folks are often physically isolated from one another. As a small percentage of the population, not all of us are lucky enough to have met or befriended trans folks before starting to consider social or medical transition. Having online spaces means we have places outside of adult entertainment to learn about trans bodies, trans stories, and trans possibilities. Breaking out of isolation saves our lives and supports us in self-actualizing.

**Online community is resilient.** One reality that trans people have to live with is the constant threats and violence against our bodies just for existing. On November 20th each year, gender-diverse communities around the world gather to observe Transgender Day of Remembrance (TDOR)—a ritual that honors the memory of trans people whose lives were lost due to

---

12   Kaemsi lives in South Africa and, until this event, had spent the last 15–16 years co-existing with load-shedding—the practice of routinely turning off power on a daily basis due to shortages and a failing infrastructure. You can see the ask video here: www.youtube.com/watch?v=hPg-3qIaFrM; and the thank-you video here: www.youtube.com/watch?v=aTcbdxFSirg. As a treat, here is the highlight reel from the event as well: www.youtube.com/watch?v=2LgBSlQjnQg&t=33s

anti-trans violence and medical neglect.[13] I have been alive—in the 2020s—for years where trans folks were scared to gather in-person for TDOR, fearing the gathering would become yet another hot spot for anti-trans violence. One beautiful thing about online community is how resilient it is. It is hard to kill us when we are decentralized and scattered around the globe. Even just within the organizing team of GenderMeowster, we have wonderful folks in Japan, Germany, Canada, the USA, the UK, Australia, and South Africa. No single bad actor could get to all of us at once.

**Intersectional community means creating spaces that work for more of us.** Being neurodivergent, non-binary, and disabled, I have done my best with the support of my friends in The Clowder (the Discord community mentioned earlier in this piece) to create a space that is thoughtful about the needs of those multiple identities. Even though I am white, we also do our best to be actively anti-racist, prioritize people of color (POC) in our fundraising efforts,[14] podcast bookings,[15] and volunteer staff, when recruiting for our Discord[16] and Twitch[17] community spaces. We have channels dedicated to multiple identities: alterhumanity, disability, neurodiversity, gender and sexuality, and plurality.

**Online spaces foster introspection through the safety of anonymity.** We use online handles for the most part on both Twitch and Discord. This not only keeps us safe from doxxing

---

13  We hold an annual event for TDOR and have also held other remembrances, like Disability Day of Mourning. You can see a playlist of all of these events here: www.youtube.com/playlist?list=PLRxYpHg9FcZAojHP_NOYVIYx_umlk8bEa

14  We use our stream team, Gender Federation, for most of our fundraising efforts: https://linktr.ee/genderfederation

15  Learn more about Genderful Podcast on our website: https://genderfulpodcast.com

16  Join our Discord server here: https://discord.gg/meowster

17  Watch our Twitch streams here: https://twitch.tv/gendermeowster

but also gives us more freedom to explore ourselves without fear of being "found out" by our in-person friends and family. Many folks have realized, through participating in the server, listening to the podcast, or hanging out in streams, that they are any or many of diverse identities. I've had non-binary friends realize they could "customize their meat suit" via HRT while still being non-binary identified. Multiple plural folks have realized they were plural in the server and by listening to our podcast episodes about plurality.[18] And my own understanding of my disability (and that I am allowed to identify as disabled) has deepened along this journey. When someone begins to understand themselves more deeply because of a space I co-created, I feel like the months of only sleeping for four hours to learn all of this new-to-me software and configuring all of it was more than worth it. The server offers more than friendship—it offers a lifeline for those who are isolated and a hatchery for those whose eggs are just about ready to crack.

**The pandemic is not over, but many able-bodied folks are pretending it is.** Now that the state-mandated lockdowns are done and vaccines are available, most able-bodied folks are back to living their pre-pandemic lives. They may have reduced their time engaging with or entirely disappeared from online spaces and groups. Multiple Twitch streams and communities have shuttered their virtual doors to return to the daily work grind. And disabled folks remain online.

**We are not powerless.** And as long as we have internet access, we are not completely isolated. The world is still experiencing, to this day, a mass disabling event called COVID-19. We are receiving those who are newly disabled by long COVID. We are holding space for the grief that comes with loss of mobility

---

18  Watch a compilation of our plurality content in this playlist: www.youtube.com/playlist?list=PLRxYpHg9FcZAOVwQYNdN3ejGQZhoDpeVf

and access as formerly able-bodied persons grapple with how ableist a colonizing, capitalist society can be.

**We cope with humor.** We share memes, tell stories, and make content to point out how silly the ableism can be.

**We cope with solidarity.** We boost each other's mutual aid requests, participate in each other's events, and keep buying each other's weird art.

**We cope with friendship.** Weaving an international web of care and belonging that transgresses international borders—communities of folks that are available to chat and comfort one another around the clock—not because we are paid by a hotline, but because we are available, and we understand that some days you need to talk, while other days you have capacity to listen.

On the horizon for GenderMeowster (the organization, not me the person): we are seeking fiscal sponsorship, and one day we hope to have non-profit status. I want to keep making gender-diverse content as a disabled person from my home. I want to keep creating, curating, moderating, and tending a vibrant, online, intersectional community that helps both disabled and gender-diverse people break out of isolation and find solidarity on their way to increased comfort with themselves and their bodies. I want to keep raising and gifting mutual aid and grant money to gender-diverse people seeking affirming care, to disabled people seeking diagnosis and/or mobility aids, and to people of color just trying to live and thrive and create beautiful, trans, queer, disabled, weird art. We are better together. Trans rights are human rights, that's right.

To learn more about GenderMeowster, Genderful Podcast, and Gender Federation, please visit: https://linktr.ee/gendermeowster

# Deeply plussed

T BORIS-SCHACTER

When I was ten years old, I got sick.

Like, really, super sick.

Like I thought it was a stomach bug, but in the morning, I was slurring my words and losing consciousness. I almost died, but instead was diagnosed with type 1 diabetes, which meant that my pancreas was no longer naturally secreting insulin (the organ's main function) and I would have to inject myself with synthetic insulin for the rest of my life.

Or I'd die.

Oh, I would also almost definitely lose my sight or a foot, which is vaguely and ominously known in the diabetic community as "complications."

As a ten-year-old newly diagnosed diabetic, I was shuffled from dietician to nutritionist to diabetes educator to learn all of the new and exciting ways I would be trying to avoid death and/or complications for the rest of my life. I was consistently told two things by all 72 of the doctors I saw:

1. I was just like every other girl my age. **Spoiler alert: It is this insidious lie diabetics are taught at diagnosis that encourages us to forget our differently abled status**

2. Diabetes is a [[read: just an ephemeral]] chronic illness

that will be cured in the next ten years. **Spoiler alert: 22 years later there is still no cure**

These repeated epithets conflicted with my newly formed understanding of diabetes as a lifelong and life-threatening illness. I would now have to undertake poking myself with needles several times a day or I would die. ("Oh my god, I could never do that!" Okay, but you would if you had to—it's just true.) I also gained awareness that I had a body, a physical form that houses my little brain and my big feelings, which was news to my ten-year-old psyche. And it was my job to take care of it because it didn't work right. My body was essentially broken, or at least my pancreas was. In 7th grade, for Halloween I dressed up as an "unemployed pancreas," a.k.a. a pancreas that DIDN'T WORK—get it? I became aware of my body and in the same moment classified it as broken and objectively unfixable outside of some mystical, theoretical cure (even though I was no different from anybody else?).

I was also going through puberty, growing boobs, getting taller, and receiving attention from men and boys in my life because of my "womanly" body. I got my period. I don't remember the first time I got it, but apparently when my mom tried to tell me about periods when I was eight, I yelled at her, "WHY ARE YOU TELLING ME THIS????" Foreshadowing the ultimate discomfort that I would have in my given corporeal form. My parents are feminists and raised my brother and me to engage with whatever we were interested in, no matter the gendered associations. I've always been into sports and getting physical and dirty, but suddenly my boy friends started treating me differently when we would play. Teachers began expecting a certain behavior from me, assuming that having grown boobs, I would stop talking so much, stop taking up so much space—let my body speak for itself. I'm just like other girls.

But I wasn't like other girls because I was wearing an insulin pump: a little robot that sits on your hip, connects to your body with a tube, and gives you insulin when you tell it to (read: Tamagotchi). My friends and I would call it Sir-Pumps-A-Lot, but otherwise my diabetes care was very private, something I was doing secretly. I didn't share it with anyone, didn't invite anyone in, because I was told that nothing about my life and its potential had changed. I was embarrassed about being different and confused about what it meant to be a diabetic. I was told this huge thing that impacts my life every second of every day didn't have to change my life at all! This compartmentalization and lack of community was painful for me. I was too ashamed to share my struggles with it. It was the early 2000s, so the technology would fail every few days or so and it would drive me !!!!bonkers!!!! and I would throw TANTRUMS from my full well of diabetic fury, lack of release, and grief for my station: a cathartic practice that has continued through my 30s.

When I throw my tantrums, people are afraid of me. I should probably do them in private. Like a werewolf. I don't wanna hurt anybody!!!! I just want the endorphin release, to let go of whatever masking I am used to keeping up that I cannot maintain when I cry—audibly, not just visibly with the silent consta-stream of tears down my beautifully undistorted face— but that actively distorted shit; when I'm alone, or in a random public place, or with a friend or family member where I can choose to let it fucking rip and release a demon or two whose name(s) I do not know.

And after 22 years of living with this disease, you'd think it wouldn't surprise me anymore. It's been significantly more than half of my life. You'd think the day-to-day vexations would not plus me. But I am straight up deeply plussed every fucking day!!!!! And I believe a lot of that is due to having been told as a child that my life would go the way I had always planned, that I would be the same as everyone else, that there would be a cure and soon. So now, when I spend an entire day on the phone with my insurance because they sent me the wrong product, or they didn't get prior authorization for an insulin I have been using for 20 years and will literally die without, I either get angry at the failure of the systems that are supposed to make my life like "everybody else's" or else feel sorry for myself and lean into feelings of "WHY ME???????"

Nobody was ever able to answer that question because nobody ever talked me through the emotionality and politics behind even asking such a question.

Because diabetics are taught that we are the same as we were pre-diagnosis, when, in these moments that jerk us into reality, we ultimately uncover that we are NOT.

It took me about ten years of living as a diabetic to realize I was not like other girls, an idea intrinsically connected to my understanding of my chronic illness as a child. Perhaps I realized since there was still no cure, those doctors could have been wrong about the other things they told me. Because other girls could drink soda, or dream of becoming a pilot, without worrying about their chronic illness getting in the way. Other girls didn't have to assess "Will I have access to the things I need that keep me alive on a daily basis?" before agreeing to a sleepover.

Through nuanced writings and readings of disability (shout-out to Eli Clare and Leah Lakshmi Piepzna-Samarasinha), I found that an alignment with the category felt freeing to me. Conceiving of my diabetes as a disability allows me to feel the fury and burnout I experience from maintaining my disease without the guilt and shame of not being able to handle my frustrations after being told over and over again that I am "just like everybody else." I had never felt a freedom within my relationship to my diabetes until releasing myself from the pressure of being able body-minded. **I have a diabetic friend who does not identify with disability and that is completely fair. But this is about me :):):)**

For a long time, I was mad at my body. It was broken. It betrayed me. It doesn't do what it is designed to do. This isn't a disease with "flare ups" or "remission"—it is a moment-to-moment dance of insulin to food to activity to context ratio guessing. I started a new job recently and I was so excited about it that for the first week or two my blood sugar would go high afterwards, I assume because of adrenaline. But who fucking knows! Twenty-two years and I'm still giving it my best shot and not necessarily knowing why or how it was accurate or off. So fun.

In the same breath that I found the language of disability to be helpful for me, I also realized that "I would be the same if I had been born a boy"; a discovery that preceded my knowledge of non-binary gender and left me secure in my realization that even though I love trans boys and relate to them on so many levels, I do not resonate with binary gender categories. I have considered hormones and top surgery ever since then—12 years. I have changed my name and my pronouns, and that has been awesome. I know there are trans masc diabetics out there who have physically transitioned, but I have not found them—I am not in community with them. I am living in the fear bubble of "your health is forever fucked up and worse than everyone else's for the rest of your life, and you are just like other girls." So when I think about top surgery, I think COMPLICATIONS. I think IRRESPONSIBLE. I think WHO WILL MANAGE YOUR DIABETES CARE WHILE RECOVERING? I think YOU SHOULD PROBABLY TAKE WAY MORE TIME OFF WORK BECAUSE SOMETHING WILL GO WRONG. I think IS IT EVEN WORTH IT????

Good news is I have figured out that yes, it is worth it, and yes, these are all legitimate questions, BUT what about the other stuff? If we take diabetes out of the equation for just like ONE FUCKING SECOND, can we think GENDER EUPHORIA? Can we think EMBODIMENT? Can we think I LOVE MY BODY AND FEEL AT HOME IN IT? Can we reconcile the exasperation and the lack of function with a desire to make a part of my body work for me instead of against me? I really would like to see all of my parts as being beneficial to me. It is a delicate balance of body positivity/acceptance and chronic illness and body modification. I was so traumatized by the anger that came up when my technology ((continuously)) failed in middle school that I stopped wearing the pump and used injections for the next 18 years. I became completely averse to any diabetes technology, including a continuous glucose monitor (CGM), all of which make managing diabetes a lot easier, as technology is wont to do. Both, however, also turn the otherwise invisible illness visible. They are both small robots but one looks like a chunky nicotine patch and the other looks like a beeper, so questions are inevitable. For almost 20 years, my shame and privacy within my relationship to diabetes held me back from using some of the tools manufactured to make my diabetes management safer and simpler.

When I turned 30 two years ago, I decided to go on a CGM to dip my toes back into the diabetic technology world—and I was immediately obsessed!! Last year, I decided to try a pump again—also fairly obsessed. I have been on it for six months now, and since I have tools, and therapy, and was unemployed for a second, I have had the time and energy to make space for the inevitable rage and exasperation. Yes, things have advanced technologically, but it still fails, and navigating insurance and being dead-named never loses its charm!

I finally made the call to set up my initial top surgery consultation about a month ago, after thinking about it for 12 years (reasonable). I didn't even realize consciously, but getting on the pump and the CGM and knowing that I have more experience and knowledge and personal autonomy in my diabetes care allowed me to take ownership of my gender journey. Realizing that this COMPLICATION (having diabetes) was negatively impacting my gender journey was an annoying and legitimate discovery. If I had gotten on a CGM and pump sooner, would I have already done this? If so, what was I waiting for?

I am trans before I am diabetic. It takes up more space in my social world. I don't talk to my friends about diabetes shit in the same way I talk to my friends about queer shit. Being queer is fun! Being diabetic is not. There are a ton of beautiful things I have gotten from being diabetic, like the muscle of advocating for my needs and verrry niche meme content. (For context: 0.55% of people living in the United States have type 1 diabetes, 11% have type 2 diabetes, and 2% are Jewish. If you are curious about the hugely vast differences between type 1 and type 2 diabetes, feel free to google!) Would I choose a life without diabetes if I could? In a fucking second!!!! I choose transness every day.

Identifying my diabetes within a wider community of disabled folks allows me to see my "reasonable accommodations" as legitimate, right, and fair. I am bringing my experience and alignment with disability into new rooms full of doctors; instead of pretending my diabetes doesn't impact me now, I will scream that it does so that I can access gender-affirming care while feeling safe. Because unlike what those doctors told me when I was ten, I actually am NOT like other girls, and there is no shame in that ;)

Written by T Boris-Schacter in the Mohicantuck Valley, 2023.

Special thanks to Floryn Honnet, Robyn Kaufman, and Nora Frank Waters.

# LOVING OURSELVES AND EACH OTHER

# Mimicry

JONATHAN EDEN

Insects were my Autistic special interest as a child. Growing up, I'd repeatedly check out field guides from the library and then go out searching for bugs in the world, identifying species with enthusiasm and lovingly drawing them in my sketchbook. These moments were full of joy for me. I hadn't yet been taught to feel ashamed of my specific interests, and whenever the moment presented itself, I'd happily relay facts about the importance of insects within the environment.

I admired how free insects seemed. Their iridescent, otherworldly bodies were an early source of queer inspiration for me, and I was intrigued by their varied ways of communicating, using signals humans couldn't understand. Subconsciously or not, I think I saw in them the possibility of something different—a world in which my gender nonconformity and neurodiverse forms of communicating could also exist as a valued and celebrated part of the world.

I was also fascinated by the ability many insects had to imitate other species.

Mimicry is a mechanism where one species resembles another or appears to be something it's not, sometimes as a defensive or protective measure. For instance, some flies mimic wasps to avoid being eaten by predators, and the large eyespots of certain butterflies and moths help them appear more threatening. Some mimics even imitate social behavior and are nearly indistinguishable from the species they model themselves after.

While insects mimic other species for survival, this array of camouflage resonated with me. As I got older, I began to learn that there were aspects of myself and my experiences that were not like those of my peers. Some of these experiences would later be pathologized in my adolescence, a stigma I quickly internalized as I navigated psychiatric diagnosis and healthcare systems. If my experience of the world was considered so abnormal, then, I imagined, the only way for me to access love and acceptance would be to perform normativity. I began to mimic the social interactions of those around me, mirroring their affect, facial expressions and gender presentation. I was afraid of what would happen if I didn't.

As a child, I didn't have the language to describe the pressures and alienation I was feeling as a result of masking my Autistic and other neurodiverse traits, or of trying to fit into a gender system I existed outside of. I only hoped that mimicry would keep me safe.

Gradually, I began to seek refuge in speculative fiction—science fiction, fantasy and horror stories set in worlds unlike our own. It might come as no surprise that I was particularly drawn to shapeshifters in these stories. In the speculative worlds I escaped to, shapeshifters were radiant and expansive. I was in awe of all the possibilities they held in their bodies. Their myriad expressions of selfhood and multiplicity called out to me as a trans child who didn't yet have the language of transness, and as a disabled and Mad person whose experiences of the world and of reality didn't always align with those around me. Like the iridescent insects I so admired, these beings offered a way out.

By definition, shapeshifters were not bound by binary understandings of the world. The rigid boundaries of gender and normativity I was struggling against didn't apply to these fluid beings, who could transition in and out of these categories with a playfulness and joy I longed to experience. I desperately wanted to be able to change as they did, to alter my form at will to best represent my inner world, where nothing made sense and nothing had to! More than anything, I wanted to be free from the expectation to be anything other than who I was, and to be able to exist in a self that was varied and sometimes incomprehensible to others.

This sense of awe and possibility turned to disappointment when I encountered stories that instead depicted shapeshifters as sinister manipulators who used illusion and trickery to deceive others. Interestingly, these accusations of deception were often centered around mimicry. If shapeshifters were revealed to be something other than what they seemed, if their true form was unveiled, they were met with disgust and fear.

I began to encounter a similar sentiment in my own world as I grew up, where it was often expected, if not demanded, that people disclose their transness and disabilities. Increasingly, I began to disclose these aspects of my experience not from a place of freedom or liberatory celebration, but because I dreaded what might happen if I didn't. If someone didn't know about my diagnoses now, would they use them against me later? If I didn't tell someone I was trans, would I also be accused of deceiving those around me?

While reading about mimicry for this essay, I ironically stumbled upon a video about one of my psychiatric diagnoses, a personality disorder I have in addition to being Autistic, accusing us of mirroring others in order to entrap and mislead them. I can't help noticing the similarity between these accusations and transphobic ones. Both sentiments view us as threats in disguise, and both ignite a terror in me, a consuming fear that my worth as a person is dependent on how well I conform to a world that will not accept me. The despair that comes from having my gender routinely misinterpreted is similar to encountering the disbelief that I am Autistic, or that I also have borderline and narcissistic personality disorder. I am told that I am too nice for one diagnosis and too well adjusted for another, or that such a configuration of experience isn't possible. Other times, I am only complimented on hiding it all so well.

These instances of misrecognition leave me weary of the world. Instead of joyously expressing my gender in the ever-shifting, otherworldly form it takes, I try to negotiate an understanding. Hoping to deter those who would misinterpret me, I once again cut short the long curly hair I am so proud of. I want it to signal something unspoken, communicating to the world that I am not what they think I am. I disclose my disability status yet again, but do so carefully, hoping that by revealing myself in a curated, palatable way, I will prove society's assumptions about me are incorrect.

It does not work, and I feel further from myself than ever.

Mimicry comes at a cost. In some speculative worlds, shapeshifters aren't able to hold on to a form for long. Their body cannot withstand being so condensed. In nature, too, there is a cost for some mimics, whose adaptability to their environment comes at the loss of something else. In my own life, the exhaustion of masking, of reconfiguring myself into a hollow approximation of who I am, threatens to fragment me.

Close to breaking, I withdraw into a cocoon, depleted and heartbroken. In the safety of that enclosure, I sleep and dream of metamorphosis.

As a child, my dreamscapes were full of agency and play. I could change my form at will, altering my appearance in ways that felt authentic and abundant instead of performative. I want to reach across time, hold hands with that child self and, together, build a portal into a future beyond gendered and ableist expectations. I want to feel the freedom of a self-expression that resists and defies definition, shifting shape as a form of multiplicity instead of conformity.

I wake and return to the present. Even though the hope these dreams inspire in me feels far away, I try to remember moments when that hasn't been the case. Through gender-affirming care, imaginative fashion and, more recently, special effects makeup, I've grown increasingly closer to realizing the sense of bodily autonomy these dreams give me.

My younger self would always choose to change my eyes in dreams, expanding their already dark color until it filled them completely, resembling the shiny black eyes of insects. The first time I wore black sclera contacts as an adult, it felt like coming home, a recreation of the visions of my childhood. Wearing these contacts has been as resoundingly life-affirming as my testosterone shots—they bring me closer to myself.

Recently, I've wanted to return to my childhood love of exploration, revisiting old sketchbooks and seeking out the bugs I cherish. I want to allow myself to get excited about them like I used to, before I focused so much of my attention on masking.

Each day, I get closer to embodying what it would be like

to live in a future-present where trans and neurodiverse experiences are celebrated instead of excluded. That world already exists inside of me. It radiates in the conversations I have with loved ones and the glimmers of possibility I feel in community. In these moments, the past, present and future collide and align. Together, we reaffirm that we are not, and have never been, alone. The worlds we imagine and traverse together are ones we're actively creating, propelling us forward—finally—towards freedom.

# Give us our roses

OLLIE MILLERHOFF

Have you ever gotten your hair cut really short after having it a certain way for a long time? Maybe you wear glasses and have taken them off after a long day? These experiences would leave you with a sensation of loss at something that used to be there. Something that used to be a burden. A necessary and, though you didn't notice it, somewhat welcome irritation. This can look like lifting up a hand to brush away hair that is no longer there or adjusting glasses you've long discarded. Adjusting a mask that had slipped. These instincts and signals that once served you now act as a reminder of what is no more.

That is how I often feel my existence to be. A once helpful, now irritating indicator that an adjustment needs to be made. When I first came out, I was a strong advocate for queer rights and justice, ready and willing to educate anyone who would stop and listen to a scared teenager. I had similar energy when I started coming to terms with the fact that I was disabled. Over time, however, I realized how little people actually cared about me, what I had to say, and the communities I was speaking for. They only cared about the optics of it all. I was being brushed aside. Like a piece of hair getting in the way.

Then the pandemic hit. People were dying. Jobs were going remote. Everyone realized that they had taken off their glasses and they needed them to see. The disabled community finally got their moment to make strides toward a world that included us. The queer community rightfully seized this opportunity to remind everyone to be wary of the government after what they pulled with the AIDS crisis. And still, when the time came for corporations and the greater population to choose between capitalist gain and in-person gatherings and the lives of those who guided them through the pandemic, they chose to sentence us to a slow, humiliating death.

I watched in disbelief with my friends and family as people all around my town started unmasking. I'd share sympathetic looks with people who still masked in grocery stores. People had started taking off their glasses again, and we who still masked were an irritating reminder that they once wore glasses for a reason. I didn't think it could get worse. In horror, I watched as my so-called friends and family, who I thought I had shared an understanding with, started unmasking. Suddenly, I found myself in the doctor's office being told that I didn't have to mask and having doctors cough on the shared computer during my pre-op. I go to the grocery store and now hear overtly loud conversations between people, wondering why anyone would still be masking. I have become something much more irritating and appalling that reminds everyone of the problem that they "used to have."

From a very young age, I learned that nothing was ever for you. Your birthday is not for you. It is for others to show how much they like you and to prove that they know you the best. Your graduation is not for you. It is about proving to everyone else that you have met the neurotypical, state-set standards of intelligence for your age group over a 12-year period. Your wedding is not for you. It is a way for others to come and ogle at an exorbitant amount of wealth spent on celebrating a contract made between two people and the state. Your funeral is not for you. It is a way for people you once knew to walk around claiming they know what you would have wanted and using such claims to process whatever they have going on in their lives over your death. Nothing, from birth to death, is for you. Everything will be made for someone else.

I have had so many birthdays come and gone that have been wasted on others. Though I am still in school, I do not see myself walking across any stage, let alone sitting in a crowd willingly, ever again. Getting wed is beyond both my interest as a polyamorous person and my ability as a disabled person. Death, however, seems the most likely out of all of these to greet me first. Truth be told, I never thought I'd get this far in life. By the time I turn in this piece, I will be 23. I am resigned to letting everything else be for someone else as it practically already is. But I'd like my funeral to be mine.

So here is my funeral. Please do not take this from me, as you have taken everything else.

Cremate me. No more fighting over what I wear or how I look. I shall be ashes. There is nothing more ambiguous than that. No more hands shall touch my body unwanted. I shall be ashes. There is nothing left to touch.

Hold my funeral on the steps of the state capitol. This place that I hate. Invite everyone to witness this life. Stuck. Unable to move. No one will take us anymore. We are a liability to their economies. At the same time, it became too dangerous to move anywhere else. They made sure we stayed away at all costs. I want everyone to see. To see they are not alone in their suffering, have accessible parking available, interpreters and open captions, and support resources for those who need them. To see that there is a great suffering going on around them, have educational resources for those who are willing to learn and help.

Make sure to invite all of my disability aids. Save them a

seat. My walker and cane, sure. But also my stuffies and fidgets. My talking cards and braces. And my meds. All 20 of them (and counting). At the end of the funeral, let those who are in need take them home. I won't be using them.

This should be a non-denominational funeral. Short and sweet. Three speeches, five songs max. For the love of all things good, do not let my bio family speak. I would like one of those speeches to be my own: I have always been terrified of death. Though I may have once been religious, for which I affectionately blame my mother's side, I quickly shook that habit and realized atheism to be a more appealing path for me. So, I was left with no answer to the question of the afterlife. My greatest fear in death is that there is in fact something after it. To say I have known nothing but pain and suffering might be a tad of an exaggeration, but then again, I was a chronically ill queer AFAB person, so I'll let you decide. My fear is that I will keep on being after death. Whether that is in reincarnation or an afterlife, I care not for the idea. It is my greatest wish that death brings an end to my being. So, if you have any prayers or well wishes for me or my soul, please ask that it is no more. Better yet, send your prayers to the living who are still suffering true pain. Pain they can still feel. That is the real tragedy. Sure, spend tonight and maybe tomorrow mourning this loss, but then do something about it. Tears without action are meaningless.

I do have one selfish request before I sign off. Give my ashes to my greatest friend (she'll know who she is). I want her to take me north. Just the two of us, as it usually is. Blasting music in the car all the way. Until we can see the whole Milky Way light up the night sky. Take me out to a field and let me go. Free to run around like I used to before I was queer. Before I was disabled. Before I was AFAB. Before I was a survivor. Before I was scared or sad or hurt. When I was just a child. Excited to see the stars glowing for me and no one else.

# The martyrdom of Saint Sebastian

ROOT HOLDEN

What could a fat, physically disabled, mentally ill, middle-aged, transgender person find resonant in the image of a Christian martyr and saint of athletes, soldiers, and plague victims? The traditional image of Saint Sebastian is a young, fit, beautiful cisgender man. He is depicted in painting and sculpture in a graceful pose, hands and feet bound to a pillar behind him, eyes gazing skyward with a body filled with arrows like a pincushion.

Historical accounts of Sebastian document him as a Roman soldier and a Christian who convinced others to convert to Christianity even in the face of persecution at the hands of the emperor. Sebastian was bound to a stake and fired upon by archers. He survived the attempt on his life, and after his recovery, he went back to Emperor Diocletian to berate him for his persecution of Christians. Emperor Diocletian again ordered Sebastian to be killed, and this time he was beaten to death and thrown into the sewer.

Sebastian's relationship with the plague-stricken requires a bit more explanation. The Black Plague was believed to be transmitted through the air and was represented in medieval paintings as black arrows. An illustrated manuscript from the 14th century details demons shooting black arrows at plague victims as punishment for their sins. The public health system and the U.S. government failed to support the gay men and transgender women who were the primary victims impacted by the AIDS epidemic. Like the Black Death, conservative Christians treated the epidemic as if it was the wrath of God punishing people for being queer.

Sebastian gazes upward to the sky in adoration or the ecstasy of pain. The vision of ecstasy and longing or gazing toward heaven, and the binding of hands and feet, also evokes BDSM culture (bondage, discipline, dominance, submission, sadism, and masochism) where the aspects of control, pain, and submission can evoke ecstasy.

The structures are still not in place to properly support queer people and have become another battleground, with conservative Christians attacking transgender health resources. I chose to work on this particular image because of the current assault on transgender care for youth and adults. Transgender women, particularly BIPOC+ transgender women, have been and continue to be martyrs on the way to equality and justice.

The needles that pierce Sebastian in this image are those used to deliver testosterone to my body. A shot per week, 52 weeks a year, for the rest of my life. I used to shake when administering my injections. The image pattern, drawn by hand, is incomplete in its embroidery, because the arthritis in my hands prevented me from completing the project. The longer I work, the more my hands tense and become painful. The drape around the genitals is incomplete, and will remain incomplete because I find my genitals to be incomplete, incongruent with the image in my head of what should be there.

# What are we worth?

LEE K HULME

Often one of the hardest things for a trans person to find is a good romantic partner. Someone who loves the transness of us, as much as the rest. Someone who will support and advocate for us. Someone who will be proud to be with us. Someone who will never treat our transness as a burden or make us feel like we should be grateful they're willing to stoop so low as to have us.

Often one of the hardest things for a disabled person to find is a good romantic partner...repeat the above.

Both of these statements are true separately, but what if you are both trans *and* disabled?

I'm trans/nonbinary/agender.

I'm disabled, including mobility issues and chronic pain.

People like me? We struggle under a multi-yoke of societal and cultural opprobrium before we even begin to get started. Oppressed. Hated. Humiliated. The first to be aimed at, the last to be given a kind hand.

We suffer social, financial, and medical mistreatment because of who we are. We lose friends, family, jobs, homes.

With all that going on, you might wonder why we even bother trying to find a partner. Or, worse, what in the world we even have to offer a potential partner. Believe me, we wonder the same. But a good partner, who understands that they must give certain things, but also that other things can be given in return, a partner who understands compromise, kindness, and thinking outside the box—that partner can turn a whole life around. It did for me.

All too often, trans and disabled folk are taught to think so badly of ourselves that we either accept a bad situation as the best we deserve or we teach ourselves to accept a life spent alone, without romantic love.

I did that. After spending most of my life not in relationships, going years between dating situations, realizing I was trans felt like the last nail in the coffin. In a life where it was already so rare to feel attracted to someone (it took being trans to also realize I was demisexual and demiace), and even rarer to find someone attracted to me, I figured that was it. The tiny number of potentially interested people had just dropped to zero. And I was, at that time, physically healthy.

The first few years of being trans didn't disabuse me of that notion, and I'd tucked away my desire to be with someone and just gotten on with things. Until the evening when a friend, Lex, whom I'd met a few years previously at university, dropped a hint that suggested she might be attracted to me. Given that I'd always been attracted to her, that would be the perfect moment to smoothly ask her out, right?

Reader, it took me a solid two weeks before I got up the nerve to actually ask her on a date. Two weeks of second-guessing what I'd heard. Eventually, just to keep from mentally torturing myself, I wrote her a rambling message: asking her out, yes, but also desperately reassuring her that no was an okay answer, and I didn't want to lose her friendship.

Then I went away and just hoped she wouldn't hate me too much for overstepping, because I still couldn't imagine she'd say yes.

Anyway, she did say yes, and we made a date. Which got canceled due to an emergency. But, to my surprise, as I sat back and figured that would be that, we began a relationship anyway, and by the time we managed to rearrange, it was really just a formality.

I was mere months into hormone treatment when we started dating, so she's been through most of this journey with me. She's also on the ace spectrum, further over than me, and it turned out that I was the first crush she'd ever had (and, later, the first person she'd felt sexual attraction for). I wasn't the first person she'd tried to date, but the first she'd been attracted to—which had taken her by surprise. Those two weeks I spent agonizing, she did too because she thought she'd made a mess of things.

But even as I fell in love, I waited to be made to feel lesser for being trans. Not intentionally—I believed she'd never do it on purpose, but people do it to us all the time, and romantic partners get more opportunity than most. But she never did.

Then came the day our physical activities grew to the point of clothing removal. She hadn't seen me without my binder at that point, much less seen what was under it (and it wasn't a small pair of somethings). I figured this might be the moment. The one where I was made to feel wrong.

I took my top off, and my binder off, and I covered myself in shame. The things on my chest were, at the time, my greatest weakness and caused daily distress and dysphoria, and here was the woman I had fallen in love with, about to gain the opportunity to hurt me beyond repair.

Instead, she took my arms away from my chest, kissed me, and told me how handsome I was.

That was the moment I knew I would never want to leave her side. Later that year, when Trans Day of Visibility rolled around, she saw it hurt me when she didn't want to share our relationship. Her reasons were valid (her family were awful people), but she saw that while I understood, I hated being hidden, so she shared.

When I had top surgery, she was right there when I woke up; she fed me painkillers and helped me do my physio. I gained a heat rash on my back from needing to wear the binder constantly, so every day she'd take some moisturizer, draw a picture on my back with it, and make me guess what it was, then rub it in. Making it a game made me feel less bad about needing her to do this extra thing on top of all the other things I needed help with, until I was recovered.

At one point, when seeing a psychiatrist, I was to be put on new medication that required a pregnancy test *for women* to check they weren't pregnant, due to the damage it can do.

I wasn't happy about it, but I reluctantly agreed to take one rather than try to argue all the reasons I couldn't possibly be pregnant (no menstruation due to hormones and, oh yeah, not having sex with a penis!). First, the nurse at my doctor's had to find a blank form and fill it in by hand because the system wouldn't let her select "Male" and "Pregnancy Test" at the same time.

What I didn't realize was that they had also written on the form itself that I was trans.

Not only was that a breach of my privacy, but it didn't even work because it was returned and they wanted another test doing.

So after Lex and I had gone to the doctor's and waited until the nurse could see us, I did another test, after the staff had called the lab and the boss there had said to write on the new form that they said just go ahead and run it.

That still didn't help. I got another call to drop by, and was told I needed to do yet another.

This time, I crashed back home in tears and draped myself over Lex, sobbing. I couldn't explain what even happened until

I stopped crying, but once I did, it was time to turn the issue over to her. The peaceful solution the first two times had been mine. But not anymore!

She called and waited on the line until she had someone to speak to. Then she calmly and firmly, repeating herself where necessary, explained that I would not be doing another test, because this was hurting me, and no test was even needed because there was no way I could be pregnant. Then she explained why I couldn't be pregnant. Coming from her, that was apparently fine, and they prescribed the medication immediately.

I knew that she would stand up for me. But seeing her fighting a battle like that, when I was too broken to do so, and fighting it in the way she knew I would want, was pretty incredible.

But what about being disabled? As I said, when we got together, I'd been fine. I was already apologetic about her having to deal with the anti-trans issues and the trans-related medical issues around me. I do think it's quite a blessing to have someone compassionate and strong to stand with me, and to hold me up when needed. But then...

It was almost her birthday. We'd moved in together the year before and were building ourselves a bit of a life. Us, pets, etc. I love getting her presents for many reasons: she gets so excited; I get to hunt down random little things that she'll take joy in and even, occasionally, something bigger that she'll love. I could wrap her a chocolate bar and she'd be filled with glee. So it's an absolute pleasure to buy for her.

I was wrapping the presents while sitting on the floor of the guest room/office, because it was the best surface I had available. All went fine. No problem. I got up, went downstairs, sat in my recliner.

When I got up a while later, it was with a scream as pain

lanced across my lower back and right down my left leg and buttock. The days of the slipped disc and sciatica had begun...

It wasn't the first time I'd pulled muscles in my back a bit, though never this bad, but still, we just had me lying on the sofa for a couple of days, taking standard painkillers, figuring it would get better.

About three days later, when Lex had to pretty much carry me to the bathroom because I couldn't walk, we realized it wasn't getting better.

A few days of prescribed muscle relaxants and painkillers later, and I could manage a shuffle, but only a very painful one. Still, I tried to keep going, still hoping for it to fade, and taking the co-codamol prescribed to me. This prescription had to keep increasing in strength as first my back and then my knees stopped obeying. Because both of my knees have osteoarthritis.

It's much worse in the left one, because I shattered that back in 2008, so my left leg was quickly becoming useless. But nobody seemed to want to do anything about it.

When we had to move, the next doctor's surgery had my knees X-rayed (confirmed: arthritis) and my back MRI'd (confirmed: slipped disc). When we moved to where we are now—and where we plan to stay—the first time I saw my new doctor, she asked about the co-codamol I was on. Co-codamol is paracetamol mixed with codeine, an opiate intended for short-term use only (three days).

I'd been on it for over three years by that point.

When she asked me if anyone had ever even offered me anything different, and I said no, she was visibly but quietly furious.

She prescribed a painkiller specifically for nerve pain, and immediately my back and sciatica improved. Not enough to be particularly mobile, especially with my knee only deteriorating, but at least enough to be manageable.

Of course, "manageable" to a disabled person with chronic pain and mobility issues is a very different "manageable" to someone without.

I'm in pain constantly. I can't walk far, stand for any amount of time, or bend down.

It means I'm pretty reliant on Lex for everything. We've had to work out how to get things done, how to split the load, knowing that this isn't getting any better. Quite the opposite as it happens—I have a recent diagnosis of a benign essential tremor, too, so carrying things I might spill or drop? Not easy!

I can't do housework: I can sit with Lex while she does some, and keep her entertained.

I can't cook 90 percent of the time: I can arrange the shopping, and try to ensure we have enough easy things to make/assemble.

I can't fully care for the furballs: I can keep the household budget and ensure we pay the bills, get the food, and try to have some spare for something nice. I'm better at keeping the mental load running than Lex is—I track everything from money to what chores need doing. She's better at doing the household jobs I ask her to do.

She's also good at doing the extra things I need, when I need them. She'll pick up an extra prescription, grab some snacks, fill my drink, and give me cuddles and sympathy when I just need to bitch about being in pain. And she's kind with me on the days when my grumpiness over it gets the best of me.

I have a great propensity to over-apologize for everything. But that's not because she makes me feel I need to; it's because I hate not being able to do things.

But she still married me. We still bought a house together. We're still each other's favorite people. When we got together, she knew about me being trans.

Neither of us could have predicted the level of disability

I'd reach, not this young. But somehow, for her, it's all worth it, to be with me.

Getting on for eight years together, she knows that she can never properly understand being trans, simply because she isn't. She listens, she learns, she seeks out understanding, but she also knows where the barriers are. She's never felt anything but cis, so how could she grasp being something else? I don't expect her to.

I need her to go as far as she can.

I need to know she loves my transness.

I need to know she will stand by me, and other trans folk, even when we're not there.

I have those things.

I need her to help me with day-to-day things.

I need her to care for me extra sometimes.

I need her to help advocate for me.

I have those things.

I never expected to find someone who would want to be with me, and who I would want to be with, long term, and that was while I was not disabled and just thought I was a lesbian. But somehow I've found this glorious thing, this glorious person, who shines on me, who gives her light so I can see.

I know how lucky I got, finding Lex. I see trans and disabled folk around me struggling to date, to find the self-esteem to try to date, too busy trying to stay in one piece to even consider dating.

I see trans disabled people around being mistreated by family, friends, the medical profession, partners, the internet...and themselves.

It's not easy, piling up all the deficiencies we see in ourselves, and the ones others (especially those we shouldn't pay attention to) see in us. It blocks the view of our narrowed world. It steals the light, it steals the warmth. It can feel cold, and dark, and pointless.

And it's true that a romantic relationship isn't, and shouldn't be, the thing we weigh ourselves against. But we're taught so hard, from so young, that we can never really be happy or fulfilled unless we have a partner, and it's really difficult to escape that. It's easy to become disillusioned when being trans and disabled means even more is piled onto this: you must have it to be happy, but you'll never have it because you don't deserve it/you're too hard to deal with/you're a freak (word choice intentional, unfortunately).

And if we find ourselves in a bad relationship, we're told (often by the person we're with, often by society, usually both) that this is the best we can expect, so suck it up.

I would like to ball up that entire concept and set it on fire.

We all deserve better. None of us should be attempting to suck up bad treatment from anyone.

I'm really lucky—Lex is amazing. Neither of us are perfect people, but we are perfect for each other.

So don't settle for anything but amazing. It probably won't look the same as the things I've talked about above, but it should feel the same. You should feel safe, loved, admired, attractive, understood, heard, and wanted.

Don't get me wrong: eight years ago, I would have been reading this with a cynical eyebrow raised. But I hope I'd still take away the message. I hope you do too.

# A love story

MILO COOPER

Foggy air puffs from my cheeks on winter nights and I think of you. I think of your broad shoulders and stubble gently shading your confident jaw. I fall asleep picturing your focused, blue-gray eyes beneath thick brows. Your deep, calming voice. Your steady gaze and contagious smile.

I love your imperfections. The scars on your chest, your elbow, your knees, from playing too hard and being unapologetically yourself. You are indecisive and messy and clumsy. You keep track of what's important, and not important, and have a hard time telling the difference. You take time for yourself, for me, for friends. You may be forgetful, but you try your best. You write things down and don't give a shit about the weird looks people give.

I carry a stack of packages down city blocks. If only you and I were strangers, walking opposite ways on the sidewalk. If only you would offer to help, so we could carry the load together. I love that you are a little too eager to lend a hand. You sometimes stretch yourself thin, but you're learning boundaries. Your will is strong for those you care about. You deserve the same protection and love.

People talk at me while I try to stay present. They try to hide their discomfort around my identities. I love that you don't talk unless you have something to say. You find silences rejuvenating, not things to fear. I love how you like to cuddle and tell people you love them. Loudly. Unapologetically. I love how you don't let your anxiety get in the way of speaking your truth and asking questions. You're calm. You know who you are.

Where are you when I need you? I half expect you to be standing in my bathroom, to feel you on the other side of my bed. I can almost believe you are here when I close my eyes. I place my fists over the bony parts of my hips and imagine they are yours, narrow and defined.

I love that you're an idealist. You try to open the eyes of too many people. At least you're trying to fix the world, one person at a time, because you know the world is just a series of individuals. I love how passionate you are, your eyes lighting up and focusing far into the distance where things are better, where things make sense to you. A place you can visit while lying on the grass with me and our dear friends. I love your hunger for learning. You ooze joy of life and take little detours to make the most out of your days.

I gag on my childhood nickname as it leaves acquaintances' mouths. Stomach tight as I turn to acknowledge. It never seems to fade. That kind of thing doesn't affect you. You know who you are. I love your name: soft yet crisp, masculine yet neutral. It suits you perfectly.

I am emboldened by your life.

I see a future where you are accepted for everything you are. Where I have faded and all that is left is this vision. Absorbed through my skin, tacked onto my soul, longing becoming an irremovable part of me.

A heat pad sits in my nightstand drawer for you and an ice-pack in the freezer. My CBD cream has long since crystallized. I'm not sure I can get the lid open, yet I keep it still.

I love you on bad days, when patience is frayed and light

is too grating. When suffering consumes you, I want to rub menthol balm into your aching muscles, to ease your pain, to make everything okay again. Or, when the symptoms linger, to lie with you as fatigue makes your limbs heavy and unwieldy.

I wish you were here.

But you are not here. Only I am here. All I can do is imagine you and breathe. Breathe although my chest is tight. Breathe although others say people like you and me do not deserve to. I am here. You are not. If I give myself time and am patient, if I promise I will never forget you, maybe one day I will see you staring back at me through the mirror. Maybe I will wear your name, and I will be the one who is a distant thought, replaced by that stubble, that laughter, surrounded by love.

Know this: even though you cannot be as perfect as the image I have sculpted, I will always love you. I will always love me, no matter who that may be.

# Bender

H HOWITT

I've always been bendy. When I was little, I'd be mindlessly chillin', sitting on the floor, like all the other kids, and someone would yell, "Ewww, why you sitting like that, you weirdo?!"— my legs arranged at seemingly impossible angles, shaped into a "W," my hip, knee, and ankle joints splayed like one of those wooden articulated toys gone slack. As I got older, I realized my bendy body made for cool party tricks, like using my arms as a skipping rope. Older still, when those super-intense hand-dryers came into public toilets, I would make my friends roar with laughter by hanging my loose skin over the jets of air, the flesh turned violently wobbly, like the inflatable air guys outside car showrooms.

I've also always been a little rigid around certain things. Since earliest childhood, I'd only eat specific foods. I could not tolerate particular fabrics, clothing labels, or socks. I refused to walk past a butcher's shop because of the smell. Strip lights appeared to me as flickering and torturous, and if I had to tolerate them for too long, a terrible feeling would bubble up inside me until I was carried out of the supermarket or department store, screaming. Sudden loud noises resulted in a similar explosion, and every Christmas my Pop would carry me out of the pantomime at the first "bang" and would spend the remainder of the performance trying to soothe me in the foyer. Despite my own rigidities, I struggled with structures—time made no sense, I had a complete inability to sit still, and the innate skill other kids seemed to have to remember their PE kit or not lose their bus money, I possessed not.

During this same developmental period, I was frequently asked by my peers if I was a boy or a girl. Around age seven, my mum cut all my hair off and my family dropped the first letter of my given name for a bit, opting for the boyish "Ollie." My sister, throughout my childhood, called me Oscar (ostensibly because I was grouchy, but the gender feels were the same regardless). I adored makeup and would frequently get in trouble for covering my face in my mum's lipstick (more Leigh Bowery than Marilyn Monroe). I had a certain innate flexibility around what I was rapidly understanding as discreet gendered categories. My sexuality, too, seemed a little loose. My main criterion for attraction then is the same now: does this person smell good to me? Gender seemed to be about the least important trait. I liked boys, I liked girls, I liked dykes, I liked fags, I loved confused straight boys, and I loved confusing straight girls. My biggest early crushes were on people whose gender flexed and shimmered, changing color in the light like an oil slick—I guess in some ways this made me homosexual.

Many years later at a queer night in Brighton, on the south coast of England, I met a special person. Their name was Frances. We got chatting and they told me it sounded like I had Ehlers-Danlos syndrome (EDS)—a connective tissue disorder—and that meant that I was probably autistic and ADHD as well (AuDHD, we call it these days). They had this theory that EDS was a neurotype that seemed to include queerness. Almost a decade later, and research is catching up with my friend. I'm one of the many who have diagnoses of gender dysphoria, autism and ADHD, and EDS. Although there is now extensive research that shows the links between autism and trans identities (my favorite of which, by Reubs J. Walsh, posits that the autistic brain is functionally resistant to cisnormative and heterosexist social conditioning), and between autism and EDS (Jessica Eccles shows that if you're bendy, you're seven times more likely to be autistic and six times as likely to have ADHD than non-benders, and Emily Casanova suggests EDS might be a subtype of autism), *and* between EDS and transness (one study by Alirezer Najafian *et al.* found that of all patients undergoing gender-affirming surgeries, 2.6% had an EDS diagnosis—that's 130 times more than the general population)—I don't yet think there is anything on these three things combined—EDS as neuroqueerness.

I'm not saying that all bendy people are trans and neurodiverse, or any other combination of those prescriptive formulas, but what I am saying is that I think Frances was really on to something. I'm captivated by the idea of EDS as a neuro(queer) type. I love the story that my gender and sexuality are bendy, my brain is bendy, my body is bendy—everything is all loose and floppy and resistant to categorization and arbitrary boxes. I love the fact that I sometimes need rigidity to hold things still for just a moment, like the straps on my joints, the leg I wrap around a chair for stability, the ready-salted Hula Hoops I have every day, and my strict bedtime routine. I'm fascinated by this juxtaposition between rigidity and flexibility, between hypersystemity and hypermobility. A sort of coming together and falling apart.

In a world where our systems fail to hold us so spectacularly, where being a bender is still life-threatening, I am reminded of how grateful I am for the ways we hold each other, the body nurturing and mind celebrating of my bendy kin; the conditions that we create for support and soft landings from our endless yielding. To benders everywhere, the ones reading this, and the ones that didn't get to, I dream of a future where we don't have to fight, where we're seen and held, a world that loves us like we love each other.

# References

Casanova, E.L., Baeza-Velasco, C., Buchanan, C.B., and Casanova, M.F. (2020). 'The relationship between Autism and Ehlers-Danlos Syndromes/Hypermobility Spectrum Disorders.' *Journal of Personalized Medicine, 10,* 4, 260. https://doi.org/10.3390/jpm10040260

Eccles, J.A. (2016). 'Hypermobility and autonomic hyperactivity: Relevance for the expression of psychiatric symptoms' (Doctoral dissertation, University of Brighton).

Najafian, A., Cylinder, I., Jedrzejewski, B., Sineath, C. *et al.* (2022). 'Ehlers-Danlos syndrome: Prevalence and outcomes in gender affirming surgery—a single institution experience.' *Plastic and Aesthetic Research, 9,* 35. https://dx.doi.org/10.20517/2347-9264.2021.89

Walsh, R.J., Krabbendam, L., Dewinter, J., and Begeer, S. (2018). 'Brief report: Gender identity differences in autistic adults: Associations with perceptual and socio-cognitive profiles.' *Journal of Autism and Developmental Disorders, 48,* 12, 4070–4078. https://doi.org/10.1007/s10803-018-3702-y

# Who fights for us...

LIOR EFFINGER-WEINTRAUB

Who fights for us when we can't fight for ourselves?

**1**

October 28, 2018, was a gorgeous day. Sunshine, blue skies, and miles of us gathered along Lake Street in South Minneapolis. Anti-trans sentiment had been gaining steam, and the action was about making our presence known. We were transgender Minnesotans, there to be seen. To be recognized as a part of the local community, part of the queer community.

As far as actions go, it was more accessible to me than many others. We found a spot on the sidewalk, and we stayed rooted to it. I didn't have to stretch my abilities and march or walk along a route. I didn't have to be more mobile than my body would allow. Pre-COVID, this was a different world for gathering en masse. No masks, no distancing. I felt truly held by this scrappy group of trans queers, singing and chanting, and hearing the support of drivers as they passed. I felt like my presence could make a difference, because there I was! In the flesh! I felt valid and like I could truly contribute to our liberation.

It was one of the last protests I was able to attend physically. I didn't know that at the time, of course.

## 2

My sense of validity and contribution has been much challenged in recent years. Since that October day, I started and finished a Master of Social Work degree, took steps along my medical transition, experienced new medical struggles, started a new career, discovered new things about my neurotype, and settled into a heart-fulfilling role as healer. And then there was COVID.

When I reflect on my identities, I feel like I'm trying to tick all the boxes. I'm trans, queer, neurodivergent, mixed-race, Pagan, middle-aged, and invisibly disabled. I feel a visceral sense of doubt and shame about myself, like I'll be accused of using labels to get attention, like I'm trying to win a contest for most-oppressed.

That's so much bullshit, of course. It's a sign of how pervasive modern political rhetoric has become, that we can think that people would want to identify as being oppressed.

Daily life as a member of multiple oppressed communities is an emotional rollercoaster. We wake up to news of legislative attacks and court decisions, hate crimes and violent deaths. We move through our days on high alert for microaggressions and slurs, little ways that acquaintances, family, and friends signal lack of understanding and care. We lie awake in bed with our smartphones, scrolling for scraps of community support, hidden between the jabs disguised as jokes and influencers looking to profit from going viral with their take on our community. All the while, society ignores our struggles and pits us against each other. Because if we cannot fight together, our fight will never be big enough to win.

## 3

What does advocacy look like when you are invisibly disabled during a pandemic? It looks like constant worry that you are not doing enough. It looks like panic attacks, wakeful nights riddled with hopelessness, and thoughts that you are letting your queer ancestors down. It looks like constant doubt that you are enough. Not queer enough, not trans enough, not disabled enough, not revolutionary enough. It looks lonely—because you are lonely, isolated, apart.

I feel like I have to fight to feel valid claiming my invisible disabilities. If someone doesn't know, they won't see it. Chronic pain is obvious some days, while on others I can move more easily. Hypermobility in an aging body becomes stiffness and swelling, and having to be careful not to move my joints in just the wrong way. I know I'm disabled, but to the outside world I often seem fine. That outside judgment fosters self-doubt that tells me I'm not disabled enough to ask for help.

Not asking for help, and learning to do without help, is one reason it took me so long to realize my neurodivergence. I grew up as the academic golden child and scholar, but now move through life as a middle-aged adult who struggles to pay bills and complete chores. As I discover more about my neurotype, I try to find balance between the pain of masking and the crippling anxiety of whether I will be accepted unmasked. Masking got me to now, able to fly under the radar and have people think I was "normal." Unmasking lets me relax into an authentic version of me, but one that no longer fits what people expect.

Classical social justice actions, where we gather in large groups, are no longer accessible. As someone with risk factors for more serious illness from COVID or long COVID, I am terrified of the ramifications of getting sick, more so because society has moved on and accepted this "new normal." It is a heartbreaking realization, to see how much my communities want to forget a virus that could kill me and has killed more than we can count. We have become acceptable casualties, offerings at the altar to the almighty economy.

Marches are doubly difficult, with too many people and too far to move for my limited mobility. Online activism feels either like virtue signaling (doing it for the 'gram) or shouting into the void. Sending letters to representatives can be effective, a way to connect without having to be face to face. But exactly because we cannot share a space with these officials to communicate our passion and need, it feels like a tiny drop in an immense bucket—a bucket that feels like it has a giant hole in the bottom so officials can ignore the voices they don't want to hear. Financial contributions feel like playing into the very capitalistic system we are struggling to pull away from. And no one of us can ever contribute enough money to repair safety nets ignored by those with the power to fully fund them. Mutual aid is beautiful, but there is a sad truth to the memes about leftists passing around the same $20 with each plea for help. Queer folks have access to less wealth and are far more likely to be underemployed. How can we contribute when we have so little energy, money, time, or mobility to contribute with?

## 4

I feel the need to acknowledge the unfairness of the burden always being on us to fight for ourselves. Martin Niemöller's words are familiar and often updated in viral social media posts to reflect who is being marginalized now.

> First they came for the socialists, and I did not speak out— because I was not a socialist. Then they came for the trade

unionists, and I did not speak out—because I was not a trade unionist. Then they came for the Jews, and I did not speak out—because I was not a Jew. Then they came for me—and there was no one left to speak for me.

It's a powerful quote, to be sure. But it is squarely aimed at those who experience less oppression. It doesn't capture the experience of those who are among the first to be targeted, or those targeted in multiple aspects of our being. It doesn't reflect the feeling of pleading for recognition and solidarity. Like urchins begging scraps from the wealthy, we beg those with disposable income, the white cisheterosexual masses, the currently able-bodied, to fight for us.

I get a sour taste in my mouth thinking of this. We beg them to care for us mostly by saying "you'll be next." As if our human existence is not enough reason for them to fight for our causes.

A lot of us end up feeling like we can't ask and shouldn't have to. And then it all falls on our own shoulders. Again.

That inner turmoil is powerful and saps what little energy I have most days. I swing through so many emotions, all tinged with the righteous anger of someone wrongfully hurt. I don't want to be the new moral panic for a country, and world, bitterly divided.

# 5

When working with my therapy clients, a common refrain I share is that letting ourselves feel joy is a radical act. And I believe that, truly I do. But I understand how sometimes it feels hollow. My clients want to know what to do to make it all better, for themselves, sure, but for all of us. I weigh how much to share about how my life and worries parallel theirs. Because I absolutely fucking GET IT.

How can we reconcile letting ourselves feel happiness and joy, in a state where our civil rights and gender-affirming healthcare are protected, when so many of our community live in states and countries that would sooner let us be fired, evicted, risk suicide and violence than allow us to live our lives? Even in my home state of Minnesota, where our legislators and governor have reaffirmed protections for LGBTQ+ folks, communities try to skirt the laws, individuals enact hatred, companies discriminate, and many of us do not feel safe. How can we enjoy a life worth fighting for when we can't stop fighting? How can we ever rest?

I wish I could tell my clients that I regularly cry, thinking of how we all feel the same feelings of inadequacy. We all feel incapable of making the changes we need. I wish I could tell them how much I love them and how much I want to throw a giant shield between them and the world's weapons. I wish I could tell them that I feel alone, that I doubt myself every day. I recognize, validate, and honor their pains because they are familiar.

In my practice, I focus on undoing the aloneness of my client's emotional experiences. It can be so healing to know that you are not alone in your hurt. Being my authentic self in relationship with a client can heal the development and societal wounds that tell us we are "other"—too different, not acceptable. I can offer them my understanding, my presence, and the opportunity to rage together, cry together, and regulate together. I can be a true, open-hearted other and help rewire intergenerational patterns of hurt. Together with my clients, we discover what secure attachment feels like and model love in ways that many of us have never felt before. I offer my clients healing, knowing that I am not fully healed myself.

I've said many times that my work, this new career of mine, feels like the best way for me to support our movements. I feel that viscerally in this societal moment. My body keeps me from the front lines of the fight. My limitations are many, so I have had to be creative. I help my community by healing my community, so that we can all continue to act.

My spouse and I have a term for when we are there for each other even when we have low capacity: tent-pole days. On those days, neither of us feels able to stand unsupported. But if we lean into each other, we both get the stability we need to do what needs doing.

My clients, my friends, and my loved ones take to the streets where I can't, engage in mutual aid and community organizing, and use their skills to advocate and educate. I support by being present and helping them feel less alone. And on those days when I can take direct action, I look for support from others to help me feel less alone.

So to answer the question of "Who fights for us?"—I fight for others when they cannot, they fight for me when I cannot. We create new ways to fight, and we share the fight. We raise our voices to gather all who care about our collective humanity. We build a future that will survive beyond fighting. And through our actions, we offer society healing, even when we ourselves are not fully healed from its oppression.

# About the editor and contributors

## Editor: Alex Iantaffi

Alex Iantaffi, PhD, MS, SEP, CST, CST-S, LMFT (they/he/lui) is an award-winning author, family therapist, WPATH certified gender specialist, AASECT certified sex therapist, Somatic Experiencing® practitioner, and clinical supervisor. Alex is Past President of the Minnesota Association for Marriage and Family Therapy (MAMFT) and Past Chair of the Trans and Queer interest network of the American Association for Marriage and Family Therapy (AAMFT). They were the recipient of the 2023 AASECT Humanitarian Award, the 2019 MAMFT Distinguished Service Award, the 2013 Twin Cities Deaf Pride Community Organization Award, the 2012 Breaking the Silence Award at the University of Minnesota, and the 2000 Best Dissertation Award from the British Educational Research Association. Alex has researched, presented, and published extensively on gender, disability, sexuality, relationships, and HIV. They are a trans masculine, nonbinary, bi queer, neurodivergent, disabled, Italian immigrant who has been living on Dakota and Anishinaabe territories, currently known as Minnesota (US) since 2008. Alex is the author of *Gender Trauma: Healing Cultural, Social, and Historical Gendered Trauma*, which was awarded the Nautilus award (gold category) in 2022 and the AASECT Book Award for Sexuality Professionals in 2023. They are the co-author of the books *How to Understand Your Gender: A Practical Guide for Exploring Who You Are, Life Isn't Binary, Hell Yeah Self-Care: A Trauma-Informed Workbook, How to Understand Your Sexuality: A Practical Guide for Exploring Who You Are*, and the upcoming *How to Understand Your Relationships* with Meg-John Barker. They also host the podcast Gender Stories. You can find out more about them at www.alexiantaffi.com or follow them on Instagram @xtaffi, @genderstories, and @edginghearts.

## Contributors

### (Team) Meg-John Barker

(Team) Meg-John Barker are a collective of (currently) five selves. They write, make zines, collaborate, friend, and engage in contemplative practice. They draw on a background in activism, academic study, psychotherapy, and Buddhism, as well as on their own lived experience. They've written graphic guides to *Queer, Gender, and Sexuality* (with Jules Scheele), as well as the anti-self-help books *How to Understand Your Gender, How to Understand Your Sexuality*, and *How to Understand Your Relationships, Life Isn't Binary*, and *Hell Yeah Self-Care* (with Alex Iantaffi), and *Rewriting the Rules: An Anti Self-Help Guide to Love, Sex and Relationships*. They also publish zines, comics, and free books on themes including plurality, trauma, consent, and creativity. Website: www.rewriting-the-rules.com.

### kitty lu bear

kitty lu bear is a white, disabled, queer, non-binary femme. Collectively, they are Mad and multiple, recognizing that their experience of "many in one body" as a multidimensional state is the lens through which they experience the world. Their literary art can be found on www.fungifemme.com or @fungifemme on the socials.

### T Boris-Schacter

T is a fat white Jewish queer crip for a free Palestine. They are currently living, laughing, and loving in the Mohicantuck Valley. Any and all inquiries or compliments can be sent to them at chef.tarlowe@gmail.com.

### Silas Bourns

Silas is an autistic gay trans man living with rheumatoid arthritis in the rural southern United States. His passions include giving life to characters, creating worlds, and telling his experiences through poetry. He crafts and develops himself through his works. He believes in disability justice and radical care. You can find him @forestantelope on Twitter/X.

### Milo Cooper

Milo is a writer balancing disability and a love of biomedicine. They can often be found in nature or on Bluesky at @milocwrites.bsky.social.

### Jonathan Eden

Jonathan Eden is a speculative fiction writer and illustrator working in comics. He is interested in using horror as a way of exploring futures of liberation, and believes every act of creation has the potential to be an act of embodiment and resistance.

### Leora (Lior) Effinger-Weintraub

Leora (Lior) Effinger-Weintraub (they/them), MSW, LICSW, is a mixed-race, queer, trans, nonbinary, neurodivergent, invisibly disabled, and pagan human, practicing psychotherapy on occupied ancestral lands of the Dakota people (Minneapolis, MN).

Their passions include helping people with complex trauma, showing up for community in creative ways, enjoying books by BIPOC/LGBTQ authors, knitting and creating art, and spending time with their spouse and cats.

## Finlay Games

Finlay Games is a transgender gay man with a passion for creating radically honest content and inspiring others to be their authentic selves.

In 2011, Finlay began documenting his gender transition and addiction recovery story via his YouTube channel, FinnTheIn-Finncinble and accompanying website and blog (https://finlaygames.com). In the years since, Finlay has spoken at several events, including the Open University s first TEDx event, 'Imagine What's Next' (www.youtube.com/watch?v=miuIUe39hcE&t=43s). As an engaging and highly sought-after speaker, Finlay aims to provide information, raise awareness, and challenge stigma around the complex topics of gender, sexuality, addiction, mental health, and chronic illness. Finlay graduated from the Open University with a first-class BSc (Hons) Open Degree majoring in Psychology, which informs the content he creates. Finlay has also written for many publications and is the author of the pioneering and candid memoir, *Top to Bottom: A Memoir and Personal Guide Through Phalloplasty*, which details his physical and emotional experiences through lower surgery.

## Root Holden

Root is a queer, trans, disabled, plural person (they/them) who currently attends the United Theological Seminary of the Twin Cities and is working toward a Master of Divinity degree in Interreligious Chaplaincy. Their goal is to support the spiritual needs of all people and create inclusive spiritual spaces for the LGBTQ2S+ community. Website: https://queerpaganclergy.com.

## H Howitt

H Howitt is an autistic artist, activist, and sex educator who was recently awarded a doctorate from the University of Brighton for their research on the sexual practices of trans people. Informed by their experience as a disabled, queer, and trans sex worker and somatics teacher, their values of access intimacy, vulnerability, creative communication, and consent underpin their creative practice. www.hhowitt.com, @DrHHowitt

## Lee Hulme

Lee (it/its) is a queer, agender, and disabled creator of stories, blogs, podcasts, and TTRPG games. It creates to entertain, inform, and help to widen the niche that queer writers get stuffed into. It enjoys gaming, reading, jigsaws, podcasts, and hanging out with its wife and their pets.

## Shanna Katz Kattari

Dr. Shanna Katz Kattari is an associate professor at the University of Michigan School of Social Work, in the Women's and Gender Studies Department (by courtesy), and is the director of the [Sexuality | Relationships | Gender] Research Collective. A queer, autistic, disabled, chronically ill, fat nonbinary femme, they are an esteemed researcher, scholar, and advocate whose work has made significant contributions to the fields of social work, health disparities, and LGBTQ+ studies. With a steadfast commitment to social justice and equity, Dr. Kattari's research and advocacy efforts have focused on understanding and addressing the unique challenges faced by marginalized communities, particularly within the realms of gender, sexuality, and disability (including neurodiversity). Find out more at http://shannakattari.com or connect @DrShannaK on Instagram and Bluesky.

### Nova Larkin Schrage

Nova Larkin Schrage is a mad disabled poet. Co enjoys cats, being a legal adult, singing, thinking critically about the world, loving, and being loved. One could read more about Nova and cos work at https://nova.repair.

### Meowster

Meowster (they/them), aka Jac, is a pagan, multiply disabled, transmasc nonbinary, pansexual, queer, polyamorous, AuDHD, wheelchair-using, white person who focuses on whimsical activism and community building. They live on unceded Coast Salish lands and have a bachelor's degree in Comparative Religion (University of Puget Sound) and a master's degree in Theological Studies (Pacific School of Religion). Professionally, they run GenderMeowster, a multifaceted organization that has live streams on Twitch, the Genderful podcast, an online Discord community called Meowster's Clowder, and regular mutual aid events with their associated stream team, Gender Federation. They love elevating trans joy for trans liberation! When Meowster isn't working on the various GenderMeowster projects they run, they like to play farming simulator video games, tend to their cats, spend time with their wife and family, enjoy witchy community, and pursue personal growth. You can support their work on Patreon or Kofi! They can be found @GenderMeowster on most social media sites or at www.GenderMeowster.com.

### Ollie Millerhoff

Ollie (he/they) works as a special education teacher in Minnesota, where they proudly hold the identities of queer, trans, disabled, and neurodivergent to show their students that being oneself can be a loving and fruitful way of life. When he isn't having fun wrangling students, Ollie enjoys reading, writing, spending time with their cat, and working on their revolving door of various crafts.

### Liz Moore (Sparrow)

Liz Moore, aka Sparrow, is a white queer and genderqueer disabled person doing their best to survive late-stage capitalism and an ongoing pandemic. They blog about disability, rare diseases, food intolerances, chronic illness survival strategies, and more on their blog, https://liminalnest.wordpress.com. They have mostly abandoned Twitter/X, but you can find them @UntoNuggan.bsky.social.

### Lawrence Lorraine Mullen

Lawrence Lorraine Mullen (they/them) is an English faculty member at SUNY Schenectady County Community College. They hold an MFA in poetry from Arcadia University and an MLIS in Archive and Records Management from San Jose State University. Lawrence's research and writing interests include gothic and horror studies, as well as archival studies, and the influences of the gothic aesthetic on the home and the body. Twitter/X and Instagram: prince_yikes.

### Jeong Eun Park

Jeong Eun Park (zie/zir and he/his) is a non-binary Asian who is an activist, writer, parent, and unapologetically not your tame queer and hyper-intelligent stoat. Jeong is a doctoral candidate of the doctorate program at the University of Illinois Urbana-Champaign campus. Zie is earning zir doctorate in Education with an emphasis on Diversity and Equity. Zie has earned zir Marriage and Family Therapist degree and has completed the certification for Sex Therapist from the University of Wisconson-Stout. Jeong is an LMFT with Edges Wellness Center and zir focus is on queer/trans/two spirit people; trauma, grief, and loss; polyam relationships; kink/leather/BDSM communities; sex workers; transnational adoptees; and sex therapy work with individuals and couples. Most importantly, Jeong is the parent of his two sons, many chosen children, and Zaza to the grandbabies of his heart, and enjoys spoiling his clowder of six beloved cats and being spoiled by his amazing partner of 14 years and counting.

### Eddy Samara

I'm a disabled queer, transmasculine curmudgeon. I meditate with my eyes open, hear poetry in broken branches, see beauty in the grit and grind of daily life, find delight in the pure chaotic joy of a d20, and spend too much of my time trying to keep the system from killing our little queer family.

### Mya Saracho

Mya is a Jewish, Latinx, disabled, queer trans artist creating work that reflects their own experience. They grew up in rural America and graduated from St. Olaf College (BA in psychology) and St. Mary's University of Minnesota (MA in marriage and family therapy). Professionally, they illustrate book covers and character art with an emphasis on depicting all bodies in queer romance and genre fiction. When not drawing, they enjoy reading bawdy novels, knitting, and dismantling the cis hetero white supremacist patriarchy. They can be found on social media as @A.LoveUnlaced.

### Coltan J. Schoenike

Coltan J. Schoenike (they/them) is a therapist, educator, activist, and PhD student working in unceded Očhéthi Šakówiŋ territory currently called Menomonie, Wisconsin. Coltan's work is largely informed by social justice principles and their own lived experiences as a queer, transfeminine, nonbinary, polyamorous, fat, and neurodivergent person. Learn more about them at their website, www.coltanschoenike.com.

## Maxwell Colletti von Raven

Once upon a time, there was a robot who dreamed of one day becoming a real boy. His name was Maxwell, and he was manufactured in Texas. His viewing lenses were broken from the start, but he muddled his way through life and became a singer-songwriter. Through lots of adventures both magical and tragic, he realized his dream and became a blind, middle-aged, queer-identified, transdude surviving a brain tumor. He currently charges his power cells with lots of coffee in a little house with his partner and family in Minneapolis, Minnesota. He thinks his favorite color is either plaid or maybe the color of fire in his old New Mexico homestead wood stove. Now he has a new dream, to play lots of dungeons and dragons, and one day, if he's really lucky, become a squirrel-resistant garden gnome.